Table of C

Content Warning ....
Prologue ....
PART 1: The Wolf Stalks 6
Back When 7
The Fracture 9
A Twist Of Sweet 11
Color Fell Off 12
The Fall 15
Like It Never Was 19
Sitting Tight 22
Echoes from the Dark 23
Tonight the World Feels Vast 26
This is What It Feels Like 29
Silence Suffers 33
Dancing for the Devil 35
Hell 38
So Heavy, I Fell 40
PART 2: Hotel Hell 42
Wander 43
Lost 45
Numb 48
Down, Down, Down 50
Behind My Eyes 52
Lit Like Static 54
Drift 57
Worth, Not Less 60
The Line 64
A Worn Novella 67
Not the One 71
Catch Me If You Can 73
Searching, in the Dark 75

Masquerade	76
Candy Shopper	77
My La-La-Bye	78
Remember	80
Forget	82
Letting Go	84
Now I Know Better	87
A Mirage of Love	89
What Would It	91
PART 3: Me, Myself, & Wise	93
Who Am I	94
Heart, Consumed	97
Uncaged Sky	99
Swing	101
Beauty	102
What Is This Skin	104
Dichotomy of Self	106
I Wonder	108
Grappling Faith	111
Grace Unearned	114
Six Was Magic	117
I Just Need	119
The Journal	121
Reflection	123
Rose Colored Sky	124
Joy	126
Hold Me/The Future Us	128
PART 4: Finding Flight	130
Hitting Bottom	131
Lost in the Jungle	133
Unbound	135
Me	138
End, Start	140

The Missed Meanings	141
Show Me	143
Elastic Heart	145
Grieve	147
Birth	149
Aura	152
Love	154
Vision	156
My Boundless Light	158
What Was It Worth	160
Run	162
A Love Like This	165
All I Can Do	167
Epilogue	172

So Heavy, I Fell

A Journey Through Wanderland

J.N. Rose

Black Roses Productions

All Rights Reserved

No part of this publication may be reproduced, distributed, or transmitted in any form or by any means, including photocopying, recording, or other electronic or mechanical methods, without the prior written permission of the publisher, except in the case of brief quotations embodied in critical reviews and certain other noncommercial uses permitted by copyright law. For permission requests, write to the publisher, addressed "Attention: Permissions Coordinator," at the address below.

Publisher Information
Black Roses Productions
Temecula, CA 92592
thejnrose@gmail.com

ACKNOWLEDGMENT

To my mom, always on her knees for me.
To those who were there when I needed them.

To the one who needs this,
you are not alone.

CONTENT WARNING

This book contains themes and content that may be distressing to some readers. Included are references to suicide ideation, rape, domestic violence, substance use, and mental health disorders. Reader discretion is advised.

If you or someone you know is affected by these issues, please seek professional help or support. Here are some resources available:

- **National Suicide Prevention Lifeline:**
  - 988 or suicidepreventionlifeline.org[1]
- **Domestic Violence Hotline:**
  - 1-800-799-7233 or thehotline.org[2]
- **Substance Abuse and Mental Health Services Administration (SAMHSA):**
  - 1-800-662-HELP (4357) or samhsa.gov[3]
- **National Alliance on Mental Illness (NAMI):**
  - 1-800-950-NAMI (6264) or nami.org[4]
- **National Sexual Assault Hotline (RAINN):**
  - 1-800-656-HOPE (4673) or rainn.org[5]

This work is not intended to provoke distress but to offer comfort in knowing that you are not alone as you navigate your own struggles.

---

1. https://suicidepreventionlifeline.org
2. https://thehotline.org
3. https://samhsa.gov
4. https://nami.org
5. https://rainn.org

Your well-being is vastly important. If you need support, remember that there is always help for you. May these pages offer you solace and encouragement as you navigate your own path to heal.

PROLOGUE

It was summer, 2022. I stood in the kitchen, heart pounding and thoughts racing—triggered. My mom and sister stared at me, their faces etched with a mix of amazement and horror. I had always been the calm one, never explosive. The details of what was said are hazy, but the deep-seated rage and confusion are unforgettable. Like a simmering volcano, I often felt a chaotic force within me, barely contained, hiding what I didn't yet understand about my disorder. Only now do I grasp the full weight and significance in many of my past behaviors. But this level of fury? It was uncharted territory.

I paced before them, my words sharp and relentless. The stress of fleeing an abusive relationship, relocating to find safety, caring for an 18-month-old mostly on my own, battling postpartum depression, reliving past trauma with an incautious therapist, balancing a full-time job, and grappling with an undiagnosed mental disorder—these were the ingredients that triggered a manic episode.

As a child, I was in and out of depression. Had my family been aware, perhaps I would have received clinical treatment. A child with a mental disorder is more vulnerable to emotional turmoil, their mind distorting reality. Paranoia and confusion are profoundly stressful, especially when the brain is still developing and trying to make sense of the world.

During my teens, I wrestled with suicidal thoughts. My emotions were a rollercoaster, with steep descents into despair. Reading and writing became my refuge, fueling my dream of becoming an author. I had raw talent, validated by many, including published authors. I was even offered a column in a popular girls' magazine. But hidden demons—insecurity and imposter syndrome—plagued my mind, destabilizing my sense of self. I passed up countless opportunities because my disorder convinced me I wasn't enough.

Living with bipolar disorder means experiencing everything in extremes—soaring highs and crushing lows. It fuels extraordinary creativity and ambition but can also drag us through tunnels of fog and despair. It's a rollercoaster we cannot control, only manage. My depression can last for weeks, and I am left to ride it out until it passes. Mood stabilizers and professional guidance help us navigate this journey because unchecked stress often triggers our next episode. Tragically, so many in the world go undiagnosed.

That kitchen experience was a turning point. My mom, a psychologist with a focus on bipolar disorder, opened my eyes to the possibility of my own diagnosis. A psychiatrist's evaluation and subsequent treatment, including mood stabilizers and finding a psychologist to work with, changed everything. Discovering my disorder and embarking on a treatment journey toward a thriving life is one of the greatest gifts my mom ever gave me.

But the diagnosis is just one part of my story and in many ways fueled it. The other part is the hard and painful journey I embarked on—the loss and shame, the rejection of old beliefs I held with unappreciative wisdom, and the embrace of new ideas that didn't always serve me well. I was unaware of the descent they would bring. For many years, I walked through a personal hell.

When I was searching for a title to tie this collection of poems together, *So Heavy, I Fell: A Journey Through Wanderland* came to me as I thought about the weight I carried and the visceral feeling it brings when you look back on your past pain and the shame in our struggles.

The title encapsulates the moment when life shifted from innocent youth to the struggles of growing up—wading through a mental health crisis, trauma from toxic and abusive relationships, friendships that both defined and pained me, and the misguided choices I made that ultimately led to much of my undoing. No one gets through this life unscathed, but some of us journey through a darker path. That just meant, as a writer, I now had a voice to share a journey that isn't just mine. They say to write what you know, and to be the authentic writer I wanted to be, I had to walk through my own pain. Had I known what that journey would look like, I might have fallen on my knees in despair. It took me 20 years to get here—20 years of walking in an isolated hell.

We all have our stories of struggle and perseverance. This is mine.

The following poems are written in a narrative arc, like chapters in a novel, with forward momentum punctuated by distinct parts. They can be read independently, but when experienced from beginning to end, they take you on a journey through my Wanderland.

PART 1: The Wolf Stalks

The cuts of invisible scars are the deepest.

Bones and bruises heal, leaving marks that eventually fade with time. People can see those scars, and they serve as reminders of what was once broken. But when someone strikes with words—gaslighting, belittling—it becomes a different kind of warfare. Emotional attacks inflict invisible wounds, psychological bruises and fractures that are unseen, yet they linger. For me, they manifest as anxiety, tension, and that constant sense of being on edge. It's the hazy memories I avoid, the sudden triggers that hit without warning, often leaving me unsure of their origin.

The hardest part is that mental scars often go unnoticed by others, and sometimes, they never fully heal. I may appear to have survived on the outside, but inside, the trauma clings, lasting far longer than any physical injury ever could. Healing is a slow, winding journey.

But when you find freedom, it never fades.

BACK WHEN

I soared beyond the skies,
A smile brighter than a desert sunrise.
Weightless, worries left no trace—
A reverse scarlet letter on my face.

When youth bloomed, I couldn't see
Innocence slipping quietly.
Back when shadows stood still,
I miss that world's untamed thrill.

My mind danced wild and free,
Where no fear could ever be.
Before anxiety stole my breath,
I miss joy, untouched by regret.

Back when being me was enough,
I miss the love—raw and rough.
Disappointment, just a breeze—
I saw myself, wild and at ease.

Frenemies blurred, friends took play,
I miss those endless summer days.
Nights where worlds were born anew—
I was light, unburdened, true.

In golden afternoons, embraced,
I glimpse her—still in place,
That daring girl without a care,
A reflection of what once was there.

The sun blushed, fears stayed small—
When school was the only call.
Now, I remember those skies,
A smile warmer than desert highs.

Weightless, worries drifted far—
Blameless beneath innocence's star.

THE FRACTURE

The fractures in my mind—
I can't trace their shape,
Only shadows slipping through cracks
Where sanctuary used to be.

Thoughts splinter like birds forgetting flight,
Wings shedding light as they spiral up,
Tracing forgotten maps across the sky.
The labyrinth twists,
Veiling the contours of my mind,
Life weaving backward through time,
Unraveling into vines that tangle my limbs.

What's truth when it bleeds from deception?
What's a villain when angels wear cracked masks?
Reality dissolves in my grasp.
The fracture? Quiet,
A splinter in my youth—a mind divided.

Euphoria soared,
Plunged into grief where light couldn't breathe,
And I, a shadow in the storm,
Laughed backward, tears spiraling skyward.
Deception danced, truth smoked away.

Chaos circled,
A circus without a center—
And I, its captive.
But through the glass,

10

I glimpsed strength forged in breakage.

Maybe these fractures aren't meant to mend,
But to be worn like armor.
We are not broken—
Just reborn, even in halves.

A TWIST OF SWEET

Ripe, tender, untouched—
Until you came, slowly fracturing me.
My sweetness stolen by your kiss,
Too young, too naive to resist.

You whispered, "I shouldn't taint you,"
But I said, "Take me."
First love, a naive surrender,
Hope slipping quietly into shadow.

You promised love,
But dust settled on hollow dreams,
The illusion fading as dusk swallowed the sky.
Obsession spiraled tight—
Lies wrapped soft as silk,
Until you let me fall, uncaught.

In the smoke, you lured me,
Promises dancing like lavender—
Gone in a blink,
Leaving only echoes.

But once, I was sweet, unbruised,
Before your kiss fractured me.

COLOR FELL OFF

One hit, he swore I'd be unbreakable,
Promised I'd harden like glass in flame.
I believed I'd rise like steel.
He said life would sing like a melody,
But fire snaked through my veins, trembling,
Winding through my spine, sinking into my bones.

In that first haze, I felt weightless,
Drifting through shattered glass,
Thinking it would lift me—
Broken wings above the ache.
We drifted in his car, a ship lost in fog.
The road beneath us cracked, the world a blur.
He said it was the only way we could be—
But the car became a vessel sailing into the storm.

Each hit left a shadow behind my eyes,
And though the world spun, I glimpsed a rainbow—
A flash of brilliance, colors I'd never seen.
But even rainbows dissolve, their beauty spilling into sky,
Leaving only a canvas, gray as void.
At first, it was a balm, cooling burns beneath my skin,
But soon, the salve turned to ash,
Slipping through my fingers like smoke.

My world leaked from a cup with no bottom,
Each drop scattered into the night.
The strength I thought I'd found became a mirage,
Dancing in the desert, just out of reach.

Joys melted like paint from the walls,
Life's colors dissolving like ink in water.
It sharpened reality—
Something to cling to in the storm.

But the storm's threads wrapped tighter,
Nooses around me.
I didn't feel the spiral—
Not until it swallowed me,
Hypnotic, distorted beauty.
I mistook chains for wings,
The cage for freedom.

When it faded, it hollowed the world around me.
The air, thick with silence,
Choked on the absence of color.
I was left with an ache, jagged and dull,
Shards of glass beneath my skin.
I chased illusions like butterflies,
But they crumbled in my hands.
I thought I was in control, but I was only a shadow,
Lost in the storm.

I felt something crumble inside,
A tower collapsing in slow motion.
I followed flames that flickered to deceive.
Truth was a chasm, and with every hit, I fell further.
In the aftermath, I fought—each breath a war.
One hit, I swore I'd rise like gold,
But I was breakable—
Shattered, scattered,
Pieces falling like stars.

It numbed me, but consumed me too—
Piece by piece, carving away what I didn't know I'd lost.
Until I clawed through the storm,
Gathering what remained.
Among the ruins of my scattered colors,
I pieced together myself—
Whole again, though broken first.

THE FALL

The first thing you did was make me smile,
A fleeting moment, bright as sunlight on water.
You wrapped me in a hug so tight—
I thought it was you, that this was it,
That all my waiting had ended,
That someone had finally come along.

I believed you'd chase away the cracks in my heart,
Like mending fragile glass.
We danced in the dark,
Our song playing soft and slow.
In the warmth, we circled in the pool,
Water lapping at our legs as if time stood still.

We built sandcastles, childlike,
Sparks in the night.
But now I see—
Those castles were always meant to crumble.
Your pain was more than you could ever be for me.

I thought I could save you,
Patch the holes in your heart,
Like trying to stop a sinking ship.
Each tear you showed me
Tied me tighter,
Made me believe all I needed
Was to love you through your hurt.

But I was blind to the truth—

16

Personal change is personal art.
You refused to paint your heart,
Refused to gather the broken pieces.
You didn't want to draw lines on the canvas;
You wanted a blank slate,
Easier to blame the world
Than to spill your soul.

You said you needed saving,
And I believed you—
That's where I was deceived.
It wasn't my job to rescue you.
You had to choose to save yourself.
I wished for love to hold me close,
But you only wanted love
To fill your void.
Now I see the truth beneath the glow.
You needed to be alone, and I needed to go.

You sank your teeth into my kindness,
Promised love but chained me in silence.
Your insecurity swallowed me whole,
Pulled me into isolation,
Piece by piece,
Until I was so small you could break me
Without a sound.

Looking back, I see the pattern—
Your love wasn't care;
It was control.
Maybe you never felt real love,
Maybe you didn't know,

But your love was possessive,
Gripping tighter with every promise.

Each word, a slow tightening of chains.
And I, desperate to hold on,
Let you pull the strings,
Thinking love was guiding us—
But it was self-hate
Weaving its web around me.

What began as euphoria
Turned into fear.
I didn't see it then,
But that was the start of the fall—
What became
The echoes in the dark.

LIKE IT NEVER WAS

I tried to forget,
Even as I struggled to remember.
The memory—hazy, dreamlike,
Moments slipping away like sand.
Was the room big or small?
A candle flickered, a poster on the wall—
But the details blurred, as if it never was.

Pushing, shouting,
Fabric tearing in his hands,
His voice echoing down the hall,
Thick and stifling, like summer heat.
Scars run deep,
The one behind my knee—a reminder.
He was no prince,
Just a man consumed by jealousy,
Chasing ghosts conjured by his fear.

His rage twisted words,
But I was more than he could ever be.
I didn't fit his world,
Naive, yet stronger than he knew.
He mistook that for weakness.

Facedown on a pillow,
The stale scent of incense lingered,
Light slipping through broken blinds.
I muffled my cries,
Guilt creeping in, cold as stone.

He acted as if it never happened—
As if it never was.

His hold wasn't love,
Just obsession—
A trap of twisted thoughts,
Romanticized and sharpened.
In an instant, the girl who shone so bright—
Gone.

Everything changes in a moment,
Like a blade pressed to skin.
I pulled myself up,
Shut down my mind.
Time blurred, love sacrificed,
Storms raged inside.
I swallowed the bitter pill of heartbreak,
But I grew stronger.

I wrapped myself in resilience,
A self-made shield.
I buried the memories deep,
Locked behind closed doors—
Easier to forget.

When love turns to torment,
Pieces of you die with it.
Better to blind the memories,
As if they never were.
Lost to the world, like I never was.

One day, when I was ready,
I faced the wounds I buried deep:
What I thought was love
Was nothing but a misled affair.
I walked through my story,
Left my innocence behind,
Broke the pieces apart,
And rebuilt with clearer eyes.

His divine mercy washed away the shame,
Like mud wiped from a window.
I closed the casket on that dead heart—
And rebirthed me.
He reminded me who I was—
A light once lost, now rising.

SITTING TIGHT

I sit, holding my breath—so still, dust suspends the light.
If I don't move, will you see me?
Hush now, don't stir—this is me, waiting for flight.

In shadows, I shrink from your towering might,
Will silence keep you from pressing into me?
I sit, holding my breath—so still, dust suspends the light.

Your voice, a storm, cracks the quiet night,
I shiver, small, aching to be free.
Hush now, don't stir—this is me, waiting for flight.

Each moment a weight—will the pressure ever lift?
Or must I remain as airless as the dust you never see?
I sit, holding my breath—so still, dust suspends the light.

In stillness, I whisper dreams of slipping from your sight,
Of breaking through the walls that cage me.
Hush now, don't stir—this is me, waiting for flight.

I wait for release, for shadows to grant me respite,
Hidden, forgotten, where I can finally be.
I sit, holding my breath—so still, dust suspends the light,
Hush now, don't stir—this is me, waiting for flight.

ECHOES FROM THE DARK

Eggshells splinter beneath my feet—
Fractured trust, cracking like time-worn bones.
A shadow clings to my skin, suffocating,
Heavy as wet silk, grotesque.

His voice slices the air, sharp as glass,
Each word, a jagged edge.
I offer my voice like a plea,
But it scatters like ash—
I am always wrong, or so the echo tells me.

It doesn't begin with fire.
It starts with silence—
A glance, a barbed whisper,
A hissed truth turned venomous.
Then the shove, hard against the wall—
How could you? You swore.

Fear thickens in my lungs,
Fills the air with poison.
This isn't living—
It's erasure, slow and methodical.
How did you whittle me down to dust?
You swore you loved me.

I watched you drown,
Your words dissolving into slurred confessions.
The bottle became your lover,
And I waited, a ghost in the shadows,

24

Hoping for the man who was never there.

You swore it wasn't you, just the alcohol,
But I knew better—
You let the drink swallow you whole.
The first time I ran,
It felt like breaking through glass,
Breathless, free for a heartbeat.

But freedom is fragile—it shattered.
The undertow pulled me back.
I told myself it would be different,
But dawn held promises it never made.
Your words etched scars into my skin,
Marks I wore like armor.

I ran, I returned,
Caught in lies that glittered with false redemption.
But no word could breathe life into the wreckage.
They say it takes seven times, maybe more,
To finally break the chains.

I ran, I returned—
But not every escape is triumph.
How many nights did I swallow my cries,
Mouth clamped shut, breathing glass?
There is no simple answer.

What held me captive?
Was it the trauma I refused to confront,
Wounds buried deep in the shadows of my mind?

Or the faint flicker of hope,
That I could salvage something pure from the wreckage
Of someone who always chose his worst over his best?

It wasn't the number of times I left,
Or the number of times I returned.
It was the moment I knew
I would never return.
The moment I reclaimed my name, my pulse, my life.

Love was never meant to taste like rust,
Or be born from shadows.
I am worth more than silence and shattered glass,
More than the lies I let shape my world.
I am more than you ever were.

TONIGHT THE WORLD FEELS VAST

Tonight, the world feels vast—
Endless, a boundless horizon.
The air is heavy, still,
Pressing down like a thick blanket,
Metallic on my tongue, sharp with memory.

My thoughts drift, distant ripples
In an ocean of space,
Where silence rings in my ears,
Broken only by unseen currents.
I search across this wide expanse,
Reaching for something real.

Every path winds through a desert
Of endless dunes—memories, fears.
Each grain of sand, a past regret.
The ground beneath me, cool and loose,
Slips away with each step,
And the air, faintly metallic,
Reminds me how far I've wandered.

A small speck, I drift untethered
Through this immense space.
The sky, vast and starless,
Deep blue, heavy and distant.
I hope—softly—that someone sees
The emptiness within,
Reaches out to fill it, even just a little,
As the cold bites deep into my skin.

Yet, somewhere, a gentle spark remains,
A faint glow on the horizon,
Like the first light of dawn.
Perhaps this endless expanse
Won't always feel so overwhelming.
I send a silent wish to the night—
Just a little kindness,
Enough to lead me back to warmth.

THIS IS WHAT IT FEELS LIKE

It's like walking upside down,
Forced to see the ceiling,
My mind twisted, bent,
The air thick, pressing in.
I fear I'll never see straight again—
This is what it feels like.

Moving forward feels like falling back,
Stained by his sweat,
As he hovers above—
A distorted rhythm:
Push in, pull out,
Push in, pull out.
I scream within my head,
As the room closes in, walls creeping nearer—
This is what it feels like.

Frozen, caught,
Mind split,
Memories flicker—
Is this happening to me?
We laughed beneath car lights,
His arm around my neck—
A signal, just for tonight.
Now laughter echoes from another room.
This is what it feels like, trapped in a dark dream.

No one hears; I can't scream.
He whispers soft, like smoke—

A compliment, he thinks.
Oblivious to the hollow in my eyes,
A force tightens around my throat,
And I'm supposed to feel desired.
A kiss that cuts,
Now shame covers me.

This is what it feels like when the lights shift,
And reality blurs.
Back at the party, he laughs with the boys,
Tosses a wink—
I'm just a toy.
Confusion clouds every thought,
Truth and lies blur into one.

Was it my fault?
Didn't we both agree?
Yes, I wanted something,
But not like this.
When he took away my choice,
Everything shifted,
A fault line cracking beneath me.

It opened the door for others—
They saw the change.
Detached, I let them take,
Numb to the pain that should have burned.
But there came a day,
I was ready to turn back,
To see what it was, and what it wasn't.

They took so much,

Or so I believed.
Now, I see the truth—
They didn't take all of me,
Not the parts that matter.
The pieces they claimed
Were never mine to keep.

What I lost was an illusion.
What I gained was clarity,
A strength I never knew I had.
I was broken, yes,
But not destroyed.
Bent, reshaped,
But not erased.

What they took—
I let it go.
I shed it like old skin,
The weight lifting as I rose.
What remains
Is who I am,
And who I choose to be.

He told me the shame that weighed me down
Would be covered with grace.
Not to erase the past,
But to reveal the truth—
They only took my belief in redemption,
Nothing more.

With Him, my vision cleared,
And through Him, I see it now—

32

This is what freedom feels like.

SILENCE SUFFERS

Time twists into a journey of loss,
Love, once gleaming, now a faded portrait,
A crooked frame hanging on the wall.
Passing the mirror, I glimpse petals—
Fallen, scattered, tossed to the wind.

"They were your choices, weren't they?
Why be surprised it didn't last?" they ask.
But they never speak of the secret pains we carry,
How, when the light fades, you're left alone in the dark,
Shadows too heavy to share.

Each day, I cycle through tides, drowning slow.
Dreams once burning bright now flicker faint.
Where excitement once caught the light,
Fear settles like dust, as if night has no end.

Inner turmoil blooms, shame clinging like damp air—
"You've got the tools to build your gift, haven't you?
Why let your life slip away?" they ask.
But they never speak of how depression stalks the craft,
A quiet predator, choking creation's flame,
Suppressing words like a friend turned foe.

Memories fray, some sharp as glass,
Others muted, washed in gray.
Thoughts stumble over cobblestones in the fog,
Frenzied desires chase shadows,
Impulses unravel with each breath.

"You're grown; you have control, don't you?
Shouldn't you own the chaos left in your wake?" they ask.
But they'll never understand the shame of disorder,
Manic twisting reality until the mirror reflects a stranger's eyes.

In these silent struggles, hurt echoes,
An agony that finds no voice, yet lingers—
A melody swallowed by silence.

And in these pains, silence suffers.

DANCING FOR THE DEVIL

Life felt like a dance on a tightrope—
Each step, a delicate balance,
Moving like a puppet, hope's threads pulling me along.
I glided through rehearsed motions,
Unaware that the web I spun
Wasn't mine to control,
Trapping me more with every turn.

I gave away pieces of myself,
Small offerings for promises that dissolved like smoke—
Tangible for a moment, slipping from my grasp.
Chasing a dream, blind to the truth,
I believed the thrill would lift me higher,
But with every spin, something fell away—
A price I never knew I'd pay.

They spun me in circles, tighter and tighter,
Until the edges blurred into nothing.
On their stage, I was a marionette,
Dancing in an illusion I mistook for real.
Beneath the performance?
A pain without a name.

Then, a crack in the light—
A subtle shift, and the dream unraveled.
Each thread pulled loose, revealing its cost.
I wasn't just playing along—
I was being drawn deeper into the void.
The ground beneath split open,

A wound I never saw coming.

This wasn't the hellfire I imagined—
No flames, no fury—
Just a slow unraveling of who I thought I was.
In that unraveling, I knew:
I wasn't merely their pawn,
But a victim of my own need to believe.

The mask I wore,
Slipped on without question,
Began to crumble.
The threads that held me
Revealed their darker weave.

I had danced so close to the edge,
Believing the illusion was mine to choose.
But now, I see—
The doorway I crossed was no escape,
But a threshold into erosion,
Where my soul wore thin, piece by piece.

I wasn't destroyed,
But I was changed—
A little less whole,
A lot more aware of the shadows
That had danced beside me all along.

Now, I see the cracks,
The places where I faltered,
Where I was led astray.

The dance was never mine to lead—
But it taught me to see through the veil,
To recognize the danger
In illusions that promise everything
And leave you grasping at air.

HELL

I didn't dance just for myself,
Or drink until the path disappeared.
I didn't trade my soul to escape,
Only to find it shattered, drained.

But you can't trust a shadow's sweet smile,
Or the one lingering just beyond the light.
You can't trust what's passed from hand to hand,
Or the spin of a merry-go-round,
Faster, tighter—until you lose your grip.

I should have seen the danger,
The mask beneath beauty's veil.
Takers will take—of that, I'm sure,
But safety beneath watchful eyes is an illusion.

Who are you in the mirror's gaze,
When compromises blur the soul's edges?
Who do you trust when everything unravels,
Reality twisting, the ground shifting beneath you?

Things aren't always as they seem—
Teeth emerge when lies hunger to feed,
Dreams shatter, fading quietly as time slips away.

In this hell, where's your escape
When sanity frays at the edges?
In the guise of survival, where do you turn,
Lost and alone, if you haven't learned?

Whispers taunt, relentless as they swell,
Echoes of laughter in an endless spell.
Where do you find solace in nights like these,
When shadows mock, tightening with every breath?

Now, standing at the edge—
I see cracks beneath my feet.
Darkness calls, a siren's plea,
But I've learned to face the light,
To reach for the flicker that fights
Against the grip of shadows,
Finding hope in what remains.

SO HEAVY, I FELL

When I fell,
I tumbled from grace,
From a sky that tore itself apart—
Slipping through cracks in a broken moon,
I plunged beneath the earth,
Into the belly of forgotten dreams.

Sank into the well where shadows grew hands,
Embracing me like lovers who never existed.
I clung to anger, fear, and love unraveling,
Each thread a whisper of ghosts.
Stubborn will twisted my spine into knots,
Dragging me deeper,
Each step a silent scream.

I reached for books made of ash,
Their pages crumbling as promises turned to smoke.
Silence coiled around me,
A noose spun from hollow wisdom.
I clutched fractured truths,
Watched them split into mirrors reflecting nothing.

Shame piled on my back,
Heavy as stone, weightless as suffocation.
Misguided desire twisted like vines of glass,
Cutting as they grew, pulling me deeper.
I grasped for anything—
But the air was smoke,
Curling through my fingers,

And I became the shadow I feared,
The darkness I ran from, now my skin.

This was my own hell,
The ground singing of fire beneath.
I was so heavy, I fell.
The weight I carried was mine,
Not a burden, but a mirror of my wounds.

I was so heavy, I fell—
Not into the abyss,
But into myself—
A universe collapsing inward,
Stars blinking out one by one,
Until only silence remained.

In the void, I found echoes,
A reflection, shadowed and still,
As if I had been falling all along.

PART 2: Hotel Hell

When Pain Meets Chaos...

Welcome to Hell, where Hopelessness and Searing Heat await. Be sure to check in at the hotel and pick up the keys to your carefully crafted room. Our concierge will gladly bring up your baggage. If your service animal, Pain, needs a place to roam, Chaos is the perfect spot—just one of the many amenities this resort offers.

Don't forget to dine at Shame, one of the city's most luxurious experiences. Compliments to the chef.

Feel free to overstay your visit; we'll simply charge the card on file. If there's anything else you require, our staff is available 24/7.

Again, welcome to Hotel Hell—we hope you enjoy your stay.

WANDER

Ever wander inside your mind?
Where walls are made of smoke, shifting with every breath.
Do those fleeting glances
Hide secret meanings, tucked away in dim light?
Or are they reflections of eyes never yours,
Mirrors folded within mirrors?

Shadows of deceit lurk just beyond reach,
Stretching, bending like liquid echoes,
As you weave a delicate web of suspicion,
A fragile gossamer strung between stars.
Thread by thread, you unravel it—
Only to find yourself spinning,
Lost in the labyrinth of thought,
A maze with no walls, no ground.
Madness? Paranoia?
Or just the cosmic dance of wandering souls?
We walk the paths we create,
Only to dissolve into mist.

Ever wander inside your mind?
Maybe the wine has blurred the lines,
Red rivers flowing through cracked glass.
Where misfits gather beneath the shroud of night,
A carnival of forgotten faces.
Swaying, caught in a fog of intoxication,
You long to escape the swirling dance,
But the steps are etched into your skin.
Madness? Paranoia?

We drift through the haze of uncertainty,
Where reality slips like water through cupped hands.

Ever wander inside your mind?
Thoughts twist and contort into shadows,
Chasing whispers that vanish like dreams of flight,
Silent wings dissolving into the ether.
Time slips through your fingers—
Not sand, but stars, falling endlessly into the void,
While pressure builds, a simmering pot ready to boil over.

Your mind plays tricks, stretching moments into infinity,
And the game? It has no rules.
Madness? Paranoia?
We're caught in the tender snare of our own illusions,
Wrapped tight like vines around forgotten ruins.
Ever wander inside your mind?
I wander inside mine.

LOST

I can't say I've never known a home,
But for years, I wandered alone—
Not on the street, but under the sun,
Searching for something I couldn't name.
There was always food, yet I starved,
Hunger gnawing at something deeper.
I never dealt in drugs, but I was hooked on false love—
A craving that left scars, hidden but real.

There was a roof, but the stars above
Gave more comfort than walls ever could,
Reminding me how small I was—
A speck in the vastness of it all.
I never had to fight,
But I learned how to be tough—
Not by choice,
But because the night demanded it.

I always had a dime in my pocket,
But time was a currency I couldn't afford.
Moments slipped like loose change,
Borrowed, never truly mine.
I had a coat, but still I shivered—
Not from cold,
But from distance,
A disconnection no fabric could warm.

I've never been invisible,
Yet I've often felt unseen,

Wandering through life,
Shadows blurring my path.
Faded dreams litter the ground,
Reminders of what could have been—
Of what I've lost,
Of what I've yet to find.

The stars still call,
But I have no map.
I walk forward,
Searching, always searching.
Yet in each step,
I find my footing again,
And in the quiet of the night,
I hear my name on the breeze.

The stars still call,
And now I see their light—
A path emerging,
Guiding me toward what's mine.
No longer lost,
I'm learning to be found.

NUMB

In the quiet of night,
I stay silent—
The drink speaks for me.
Numbness wraps around,
Thick fog, heavy and dense.

Before dawn,
I avoid the mirror—
The drink, my refuge.
Numbness brings calm,
A fleeting balm.

In solitude,
I suppress my voice—
The drink, my comfort.
Numbness dulls the pain,
Blunts the edge.

In restless thoughts,
I push worry away—
The drink, my shield.
Numbness quiets the storm,
Hushes the rage.

But with morning's light,
I find my voice—
Words spill, raw and true.
Numbness reveals itself,
A silent thief, a cruel disguise.

In daylight's glare,
I face the shadows,
Wrestling with darkness
That numbness hides.

In the sun's warmth,
I let my voice rise,
Breaking free from silence,
A melody deep and wide.

In the breeze of a new day,
I scatter my fears like leaves.
Freedom blooms,
With the courage to feel.

In life's fullness,
I choose to care—
Heart and soul, entwined.
Strength rises,
Like the dawn, renewed and bright.

DOWN, DOWN, DOWN

I keep sinking—down, deeper still,
Like a leaf caught in a storm, with no ground to hold me.
Tears fall, but they vanish into the wind, unnoticed.
Down, down, down—
Let the darkness cradle me.
Though I'm already here, it's never silent.
The thoughts linger:
There's nowhere but down to go.

Yes, there is.

I keep sinking,
My tears fall like rain, unnoticed.
And the thoughts continue:
There's nowhere but down to go.

Yes, there is.

In that darkness, I miss the hand that taps my shoulder;
I turn away from the whisper, softer than the rest.
So wrapped in the thought that I am just wrong,
I don't feel the quiet hug that softly says:
"Stay, you do belong.
And when you're lost in the sadness, just hold on to Me."

When I pause, just for a moment,
I realize I'm not alone.
I listen to the voice,

Reaching for the thread of hope,
To climb up, up, up.
Holding on to the belief
That peace will find me,
A calm I can finally hold on to.

"I promise, just hold on to Me."

BEHIND MY EYES

I could smile without smiling,
Laugh without laughter,
Open yet hiding within—
A paradox in plain sight.
But you had to draw close
To truly see the world behind my eyes.

I spun pretty words with ease,
Crafting tales where truth blurred with lies.
Hard things spilled like dark confetti—
Fragments of pain scattered in time,
While hidden tears lingered,
Just out of sight, behind my eyes.

Life of the party—I dazzled,
Winking without winking,
Mixing signals, teasing the truth,
Keeping it at bay.
Yet unseen tears cascaded freely,
Veiled where no one looked—behind my eyes.

Lost in thought, hard to read,
I played loud music to drown the noise,
Buried thoughts in books to quiet the mind.
But in the stillness, echoes resounded,
Reverberating behind my eyes.

I yearned to connect,
But words never told it all.

Struggling to let anyone in,
I penned my thoughts in midnight's grip,
Where chaos spun in brilliance,
Unveiled behind my eyes.

You might remember me as kind,
But even soft smiles can break.
To truly know me, you'd need to be gentle—
For within, a silent war raged,
Unseen and relentless, I was fading,
Slowly disappearing behind my eyes.

If I've fallen behind my eyes, where have I gone?
And why don't we cry for help when we need it?
Has the world shrugged its shoulders too many times?
Maybe that's how it feels.

How can you trust someone to hold
Your hand and never let go?
All the pain that hid behind my eyes,
I never thought anyone could understand.
Maybe the world should listen more,
Stop to feel the quiet cries.
We say humanity is about life,
But what is life when our hearts
Are dying inside it?

If we just paused to listen,
To look past ourselves for a while,
How many lives, quietly taken, could be saved?
How many souls, still hanging on,
Could find a way to breathe?

LIT LIKE STATIC

They were my wild friends,
Silent partners in midnight pacts,
Pulling me into the hum of the night—
Grainy film flickers, reel spinning fast,
Twenty-five, charged with static,
Running on time we couldn't grasp,
Thinking we'd last forever.

Glitter-clad and defiant,
We danced on the edge of youth,
Silhouettes in neon dreams,
Shadows stretching beneath the moon's gaze.
Fiery eyes, lipstick bold, lashes sharp—
Bravado with no disguise.

Neon nights, heels clicking,
Laughter sharp as crystal,
Flashing grins daring the light,
Drinks in hand, sparks flying fast.
Volume high, the night a blur,
Lights and motion, a dizzying whirl.

Through crowded bars we moved,
Swaying, pulling,
Scanning the crowd for a spark—
To ignite the night, to delay the dawn.
Accomplices in a reckless plot,
Knowing smiles exchanged,
The shot lingers.

Intoxicated, revelry blurred,
Mirrors reflecting our fleeting pride.
Heels tapping on sticky floors,
Laughter shared through iridescent eyes—
"Hey girl, you alright?" we'd slur.
The scene cuts black, echoes stir.

Looking back on those lightning nights—
If I could rewind the reel, I'd say:
You pulled me out; we sang our script.
On nights when I was low,
You knew, though not how deep,
But still, you pulled me close.
We laughed, caught in our young adult glow.

There's nothing like the magic
Of girls under silver screen skies.
You said something was in the air—
It was the beauty of a galaxy aware,
No stars brighter than those in real friendship.

We were the unrivaled cast,
Moments strung together
By the lines of our anthems,
Asking the sky for more.
But slowly, without us knowing,
The light began to fade.
Brilliance that once blinded us
Softened, dimmed,
Like stars pulling back at dawn.

Gone before we felt the shift,
And oh, how time can be so cruel—
Turning stars into memories,
Credits rolling quietly,
Marking
The end.

DRIFT

I've been circling you,
Like a moon caught in your gravity,
Hoping—perhaps foolishly—
To feel your pull,
To glimpse the warmth
That once tethered me close.

All I needed was a signal,
A flare in the dark,
But your light grew distant,
Fading into the void.
I kept spinning,
Trying to align our paths,
But you—
You let the silence stretch,
Let the distance grow,
Left me floating,
Lost in this cold, vast expanse.

I watched stars burn out,
Wished on their dying light,
But even the cosmos stayed silent.
I waited for you
To change course,
To pull me back in,
But you drifted further,
Leaving me to navigate
This endless dark alone.

And I wonder—
Was it just you?
Or was I too wrapped in my own orbit,
Too afraid to slow down,
Fearing what stillness might reveal?

I've been a rogue planet,
Unmoored,
Searching for the gravity
We once shared.
But you—
You kept your distance,
Let the space between us
Become infinite.

Now, I gather fragments,
Pieces of what we were—
Shattered stars,
Broken constellations,
Trying to find patterns
We lost.

In the quiet,
In the stillness of the cosmic dark,
I see it now—
It wasn't just the universe that drifted,
It was us—
We let go,
Lost the gravity
That kept us close.

Here I am,

Keeping me trapped in limbo,
Wishing for more, always.

I tried to bury myself in noise—
Drink, dance, repeat.
But the joy rings hollow,
Every laugh feels thin,
And your touch lingers,
An unwelcome ghost I can't shake.

Even in sleep,
There is no peace.
I toss,
I turn,
Haunted by memories of you.
I wait for your voice,
Though I know it's an empty call.
An empty voice.
An empty me.
Empty.

And when I gather the strength to let you go,
It's as though you know,
As though you feel it.
Suddenly, you reach out,
And the sound of your voice pulls me back in—
So real, so familiar.
I fall for it every time.

I forget, once again,
That I'm just the girl you call
When night falls.

Chasing after something as fleeting as smoke—
Impermanence.
Here I am, breaking my own heart for trying.
In the haze, I forgot—

I forgot how important I am.
That I'm human too,
Not just your plaything,
Not some background character in your story.

If only I had shifted my gaze,
Looked beyond you,
Peeked behind the veil of your charm.
Maybe then I'd understand
Why I believed I didn't deserve a better dance.

But now,
Now I see.
I take my younger self's hand,
Pull her close,
And I teach her.
I'll show her that the love she seeks
Is not beyond her,
But within.

I'll teach her what she never knew—
That shame doesn't define her,
That losses can carve her into wisdom.
Whatever weight she carries,
I'll show her how to lay it down,
How to find herself again.
She'll see her beauty,

Restored,
Reborn,
Once more.

THE LINE

I said there was a line I wouldn't cross.
On the drive over,
Anticipation hums—
Like the air before a storm.
I shouldn't be on this street,
Shouldn't be heading this way,
But here I am—
Drawn in, electric,
Alive with the promise
Of something forbidden.

You greet me at the door—
Too familiar.
I've always had that thing about me.
They always want more.
But if I cross the threshold,
What does that make me?

Family photos line the walls—
A perfect life,
Untouched.
Pasta simmers on the stove,
Shoes lined up, big to small.
Everything in order,
Except me.

He pops the cork—
Practiced,
Like someone who knows the game.

I shouldn't be here,
But the thrill—
There's nothing like it.

Skating the edge,
I feel feral,
Alive.
But I haven't crossed.
Not yet.
The calm masks the chaos beneath—
That's what calls to me.

Magnets smile from the fridge,
As I weigh the risks.
He offers a tour,
As if I haven't been here before.
But never alone.

The house watches,
Its walls silent,
Shadows like knives.
I could still leave—
I've always been good at slipping away.
Practice makes perfect, doesn't it?

Nervous laughter,
The sun sinks lower.
Time presses in,
Tightens its grip.
And I feel it—
That familiar pull.

Her perfume lingers in the hall,
Laundry undone, a soccer ball kicked aside.
The wine blurs my senses,
Dulls the signs of lives lived here.
I'm the intruder,
The spark,
Answering a call that isn't mine.

Then—
A voice inside, quiet but clear,
Whispers: Go.
I glance around the room,
My body too still on the bed.

The voice grows louder: Go.
I know this line can't be uncrossed.
Not after this.

Still, I hesitate.
Still, I waver.
Go.

Some lines, once crossed,
There's no return.
And I know—
Even if I have to run,
Even if my head hangs low,
I'll be grateful.
Because this I almost lost:
I said there was a line I wouldn't cross.

A WORN NOVELLA

Chapter 1: The Beginning
The city hums in shades of gray,
Neon flickers like ghosts caught in the rain.
Wind slips through my hair—a fleeting caress,
Too faint to fill the void gnawing inside.
I glide through the night, untethered,
As if I could outrun the ache that always lingers,
A step behind.
Another chapter opens, scrawled in the margins
Of a story I never chose to read.
"Where are we going?" My voice shivers,
Though the question feels hollow.
His words wrap around me,
Velvet promises that dissolve by dawn,
Like ink bleeding on a page too worn from turning.

Chapter 2: The Plot Thickens
His hands mold me like clay,
Shaping me into a silhouette he's traced before—
Familiar, rehearsed.
We dance at the edge of the night,
Spinning in circles we'll forget by morning.
Tomorrow, he'll leave me in the shadows
Of a plot that leads nowhere.
"No rush," he murmurs,
As if time could bend for us,
Stretch until it breaks.
But I know this scene—
The thrill dissolves with daylight's indifference,

Another twist leading back to the start.

Chapter 3: The Interlude

I'm a mannequin draped in simplicity,
Just another line in his script.
Silk kisses my skin, cold as the emptiness beneath.
The sharp tang of wine lingers—
A bitter pause between acts,
Punctuation that stings.
I know this story. I've lived it too many times—
The same script, the same lines.
Yet I play my part,
Knowing I'm barely in it.

Chapter 4: The Climax

"You're mine," he whispers
As the night folds around us like a closing book.
But even as he speaks, I feel the moment slipping—
Unraveling, smoke through my fingers.
I know the ending—it's always the same.
But this time, something shifts.
I used to believe I had to play along,
That the story could never change.
Yet now, with every breath,
The script feels thinner,
The lines weaker.
I lie awake,
The weight of this story pressing down,
Heavy and suffocating.
The moon watches, silent and cold,
As we replay the prose,
Line by line,

The plot thinning by the minute.
Suddenly, I know—
I can't keep living this narrative.
The ending was never mine.
I want out.

Chapter 5: The Resolution
I stare into the mirror at the girl who's played this role too long.
"You're better than this," I want to say.
I am better than these lines that cage me,
Better than the roles I've been cast in.
The story I've been living was never mine.
It was borrowed, stolen even.
I was an actor on a stage I didn't choose,
Bound by someone else's script.
But now, I'm ready to rewrite the ending.
I want to find something real,
Something that doesn't fade with the dawn,
Something that's mine.
The roles I've played, the lines I've followed—
They served their purpose.
They showed me what I don't want to be.
I'm done being a character in someone else's story.
The plot ends here.

Epilogue: The New Beginning
I toss the old script aside, stepping from its shadow.
This time, I write the story.
The pages are mine—blank, waiting for my hand to shape them.
No longer the supporting role, I'll craft a narrative that lasts.
This time, I'm more than enough.
And this ending?

It's entirely mine.

NOT THE ONE

I won't follow your lead.
You conjured shame, played your petty game—no longer.
You presumed you could command this dance—try it.
But soon you'll know: I'm not the one, not tonight.

We stepped into a wretched waltz,
Yet I was never yours, merely a fleeting illusion.
You mistook my gentleness for frailty,
But my heart beats with embers,
And my spirit pirouettes in fierce liberty.

I glide like ice over this floor,
Cutting through the fabric of your lies.
You thought I was an effortless partner,
Misinterpreting the tempo,
Taking my silence as acquiescence.

You boasted, yet I am not your conquest;
I am the dark swan's final pirouette,
The closing note in a symphony you'll never forget.

Go ahead, attempt to lead.
I'll spin you too near the sun,
Watch you stumble and burn.
Feel the scorch of every forced step,
Every motion that sought to diminish me,
Only to stoke a fire you cannot extinguish,
A rhythm you cannot govern.

You won't forget this dance,
Won't forget my name.
I am the tempest in your tango,
The storm that unsettles your ground,
The echo of your missteps,
A reckoning long overdue.

What did you expect?
A docile partner?
No.
I am the wildfire in this dance,
The force that shifts the earth beneath you,
And tonight, you'll remember my name.

CATCH ME IF YOU CAN

Catch me if you can—
I'm the spin in your mind,
The echo in the cave,
The shadow slipping away.
Fair game?
No deals here.
This is manic's chase, and I'm in deep.

Desire flares like lightning in a storm,
I leap from bed to bed,
Leaving whispers behind.
Maybe I'll remember—maybe I won't.
Manic's at the wheel, skipping lines,
And when I'm high on this ride,
The Ferris wheel spins too fast—
Weightless at the top,
But the drop pulls me under.

Need a shopping spree? Let's go.
Impulse tingles my skin,
Money slipping like water.
Manic's in control,
A heartbeat from breaking,
Just a breath from losing it all.

You think these moments are fleeting,
But they stretch like endless nights,
A reel spinning slow...
Caught in the loop, manic's the director,

And I'm just reciting my lines.

The worst part?
In this scene, I'm the only one.
Ever wonder what chaos feels like?
Words trip over themselves,
Wading through fog,
Shattering bonds like glass.
Thoughts splinter like broken light,
Nothing sticks, nothing fits.

If I could slow down, I would,
But chaos is relentless,
And I'm trapped in its grip.
Trapped, I dread waking to wreckage,
Aware, yet powerless to fix the damage.
An imposter in my own life—
That's how it feels.
Who I am and who I'm not,
A puzzle with shifting edges,
Pieces scattered, never fitting.

Guilt hangs heavy where I stand,
Caught between the person I am
And the one they expect.
I wish you could catch me,
Because I'm running wild in this landscape.
I know I can be many things,
But I'm spinning without a guide.

So catch me—if you can.

SEARCHING, IN THE DARK

In darkened nights, my frustration howls into the void,
I seek a whisper, a sign to light my way.
Unpredictable as Russian roulette, I am lost in the night.

Truth hides in shadows where doubt is employed,
Answers slip through silence; hope begins to sway.
In darkened nights, my frustration howls into the void.

I sift through echoes, each breath near destroyed,
A heart that yearns for more than words can say.
Unpredictable as Russian roulette, I am lost in the night.

Maps turned to riddles, their meanings alloyed,
Yet still I search, though the darkness holds sway.
In darkened nights, my frustration howls into the void.

I trace fading stars where lost dreams once toyed,
A mind untamed, chasing light's distant ray.
Unpredictable as Russian roulette, I am lost in the night.

No compass, no savior, no truth yet deployed,
But still, I reach, through each question's dismay.
In darkened nights, my frustration howls into the void,
Unpredictable as Russian roulette, I am lost in the night.

MASQUERADE

In the circus of clowns, where joy is a guise,
Grins painted on, hiding truth in disguise.
I sought refuge behind gaudy tents,
But found only a parade of false pretense.

Mirrors stretch and warp my inner self,
Reflecting shattered dreams on dusty shelves.
I'd rather sink beneath the weight of truth
Than dance to the ringmaster's mocking sleuth.

Among the clowns, the laughter rings hollow,
I find my escape in the quiet that follows.
The tent flaps whisper of freedom, of flight,
Guiding me out from shadows to light.

No longer a puppet in this carnival's play,
I sever the strings that kept me at bay.
Beneath the big top, a revelation unfolds—
A self rediscovered, no longer controlled.

Farewell to the fanfare, the charade at its end,
To the ringmaster's call, I will not bend.
Stepping from under the weight of deceit,
I walk into dawn, my soul complete.

With each step away, the circus grows dim,
A chapter concluded on a whimsical whim.
Ahead lies the truth, stark in daylight,
Far from the echoes of the carnival's plight.

CANDY SHOPPER

A spoonful of sugar helps the lies go down,
Turning bitter into sweet, a candy-coated crown.
Your words, so rich they twist on my tongue,
Like licorice, they linger long after they're spun.

They scatter in my mouth like pop rocks,
A kiss that stains like a lollipop.
I thought your smile was too vanilla,
A laugh smoother than frozen yogurt in summer.

Your mind's a candy shop, a tangle of sweet things,
Spitting out words like gumballs in bright rings.
From all your manufactured sugar, I've got cavities,
Yet I'm hooked on your drops of truth, like jelly beans.

You wrap around me like bubblegum tape,
I dole out pieces of myself like birthday cake.
You savor my flavor like a Jolly Rancher,
Cotton candy clouds my head—this sugar high's a dancer.

But soon, the sweetness starts to sour,
I reject your sundaes, topped with cherries, hour by hour.
Caught in your spin, like a gobstopper I whirl—
Just another candy shopper, lost in your swirl.

I'll be sick off your syrup before too long,
Stepping away from your sugar-coated song.
No more candy high, no more bitter beneath—
I'm done with the sweetness hiding the teeth.

MY LA-LA-BYE

Cue the violins, the keys start to sway,
In E major begins your soft dismay.
You weave a tale of the world turned gray,
Of battles lost, of dreams led astray.

An unseen Robin Hood, cloaked in your pleas,
Your murmured woes, like whispers through trees.
I thought I could lift you,
Raise you up high,
Thought I could heal you—
But it was all a lullaby,
Sweet on the surface, hollow inside.

Then the bough broke, and down came the fall—
I saw through the cracks in your paper-thin wall.
Craving the love you never knew,
But you're no child, and I'm not here to rescue you.

You're a grown man, not a babe in a crib,
And I'm no shepherd for the fears that you hid.
I crave something more, a life that's my own,
Not just a nurse, caught in your undertone.

I listen to your melody,
The rhythm you play,
The verses you hum—
But they fade away.

One day, I'll sing to you,

A lullaby both tender and sly.
You'll hear the truth in every line,
And as the echoes fade, you'll wonder why—

Regret will find you in the quiet of night,
When my La-La-Bye closes the door,
Leaving you to face your own night.

REMEMBER

Do you remember when I eagerly awaited your voice,
Our laughter endless, timeless, as if nothing else mattered?
You knew, even then, how deeply I'd fall—
Do you remember when that summer was ours,
Each moment together, as if we had all the time in the world?

Do you remember taking me out, teaching me to drive stick?
When I stalled, and we laughed until tears blurred the night?
Our laughter echoed through the stillness, filling the air.
That park where we'd listen to music in your car—
Do you remember pointing out the stars,
Tracing constellations with your finger,
Mapping out a future we thought was written in the sky?

Do you remember holding my hands,
Admiring their length, their strength?
When you let me into the quiet corners of your thoughts,
Do you remember playing your guitar,
Saying that with me, your lyrics finally had a place to belong?

Do you remember picking me up after curfew,
Sneaking away under the cover of night?
The first time you lit that candle, and we kissed—
Do you remember how you looked at me then,
Promising we'd savor every moment,
Lying afterward, face to face, toe to toe,
As if the world had shrunk to just us?
Do you remember the places our adventures took us?

The miles that stretched between us,
How we counted the days until we were together again?
Do you remember the weekend visits,
Reminiscing about the past, dreaming about the future,
Sharing secret wishes only we knew?

Do you remember how, one day, without a word,
You just... disappeared?
You never said goodbye.

FORGET

I'll miss the kisses you pressed to my neck,
The warmth of summer's golden embrace,
Your touch, soft and gentle,
Fluttering like butterflies in delicate flight.

I'll miss how we once fell through starlit skies,
Landing softly where dreams quietly rise.
I'll miss reaching for you in the stillness of night,
In those hushed moments when our love would ignite.

I still feel your gaze, lingering,
Sense your breath, tender and near.
In those early days, your touch was a promise,
A quiet vow, light as air.

But even then, shadows whispered at the edges,
And love, once pure, began to fray.
I hold on to the memory of what we were—
Before the darkness crept in,
Before tenderness turned to pain.

I cling to those first touches, so true,
Knowing that in time, I'll learn to let go.
One day, the ache will soften,
Like a scent drifting on the breeze.

But even as the pain fades,
And peace finds me at last,
I'll carry the sorrow of love lost,

Cradled in whispers from the past.

LETTING GO

Letting you slip away is like catching smoke—
No clean break, no final word.
In silence, I recall laughter under stars,
Your touch, a breeze, our whispered vows.
We danced through darkness, shadows entwined,
The world shrinking to fit our hands.
Yet memories deceive; sweetness turns to salt.
Warmth fades, and cold truth takes hold:
You linger still, slipping through walls,
A phantom haunting quiet corners.

In our child's eyes, I trace your reflection,
A smile I still cherish—
Yet shadows seep beneath the light,
Fragments I long tried to forget.
The kettle shrieks your name into silence,
A text's ping morphs into echoes.
Sweet words that concealed sharp edges.
I step into the Jeep; your scent clings,
But forget how you steered me toward the edge.

The fridge murmurs—two spoons, not three,
Yet I forget how you emptied it with lies.
The jokes we spun shatter like brittle glass,
Your laughter reverberates, tinged with shadows,
And I played along, blind to the dark.
When the lights fade, the room warps—
I'd rather blackout than confront our montage.
For goodbye is never truly goodbye; it lingers,

A toothache gnawing beneath my ribs,
Pulsing through bones that remember too well.

The truth is this: you carved a fissure in my spine,
My heart sinking in quicksand, slipping from reach.
How do you carry the weight of a ghost—
Shifting, fading, yet never light enough to release?
How do I unlearn the bruises beneath the sweet?
They say time erases, but it only liquefies.
Love bleeds like ink into water,
Staining all I believed was pure.
Perhaps you'll rise from your own ashes,
And I will unravel, thread by thread—

So when you return,
We might align like fractured puzzle pieces.
But I know the edges now.
Memories twist, lose their grip,
Blurring the line between best and worst.
And through it all, I stand, unbroken,
Free to embrace this unfamiliar liberation—
A life forged from what we shattered.
A love that lingers, yet no longer binds.
And now, I turn to the open sky,
Embracing the air, untethered and light,
Stepping into freedom—toward a life
Where I am no longer anchored to you.

I let you dissolve into mist—
To unearth the bones buried beneath your weight.
Not always kind; your voice unraveled the seams.
Your love stained; you never learned how—

Perhaps, neither did I.
The weight of missing you presses on my chest,
But I let it fall, let it slip away.
Releasing you feels like shedding armor—
Yet the lightness brings an unexpected relief.

Perhaps this heaviness,
The one I carried through sleepless nights,
Was all I ever knew.
Yet this isn't truly goodbye.
We share the child, the mirror, the ghost of us.
Letting you go softens the edges of longing.
The past melts into itself—
And finally, I am free—
Free to break from your shadow,
And blaze a path of my own design.
Free,
To give myself
This strange, unburdened gift.

NOW I KNOW BETTER

You didn't mean to break me down,
But the weight of your pain unraveled my seams.
Your words, once soft, began to cut,
Carving through the dreams we shared.

You brought shadows you never intended,
Tried to find your strength in the chaos,
But here I stand—still whole,
Even as you lost yourself along the way.

Your laughter echoed, but it wasn't you,
Just the hollow shell that addiction built.
I met your gaze, searching for the man I knew,
But all I saw were cracks in the armor you wore.

I should have held my worth closer,
Cradled it like the precious gem it is.
Yet I let you in, believing you'd find your way back.
Now the fog has lifted, and my value shines—clear, untarnished.

You pulled me into your cycles,
Spoke of love while wrestling your own demons.
But your words, no matter how sincere,
Could never quiet the storm inside you.
You weren't the villain I painted,
Just a soul lost behind walls you couldn't tear down.
I see that now, the drama was never all you—
It was the battle you fought alone,
And I was collateral in your war.

I should have cherished myself,
Built my esteem into something unbreakable,
But I hoped for your redemption instead.
Now, I've found the truth, and I'm finally free.
Though I've reclaimed my time, my dreams, my light,
I see the man you once were—
And for a while, you were lucky to have me,
Even as you slipped away.

A MIRAGE OF LOVE

Love, I thought, was in that look—
A flirty grin, the clink of glasses at ten.
In those moments, I felt alive,
Revived, as though something new had been born.
But just as quickly, the loneliness returned—
Joy, borrowed, fleeting,
Gone as swiftly as it came.

One moment, I was weightless, soaring,
The next, the heaviness of emptiness
Settled in like an old companion.
Looking back, I see it wasn't love—
Just a mirage I chased,
Reflections of desires unmet,
Illusions softening the edges of my sight.

True love, I've come to know,
Doesn't vanish like a wisp of smoke,
Doesn't live in the brief sparks
That catch the eye
But fail to light the soul.
All those dreams I once held
Of what love could be
Faded like mist clinging to dawn,
Fantasies I clutched for too long.

You can't close your eyes when you dream—
You'll miss the wonder happening
Right before you.

As days blurred into nights,
Seasons turned their slow, steady arc,
My heart began to see:
Love's essence doesn't dwell in the thrill
But in the quiet glow that deepens with time.

When the shimmer fades,
Real love rises, slow and steady,
Enduring.

WHAT WOULD IT

What would it feel like to have a partner who truly listens,
Walking hand in hand,
Not just in step but in spirit,
Moving through life with shared dreams and whispered wishes?

What would it feel like to be protected,
To have someone cradle your heart with care,
Guarding your secrets not as weapons,
But as treasures—sacred and rare?

What would it feel like to be loved,
Unconditionally, for who you are,
To stand before someone who truly sees you,
Understanding every hidden scar?

What would it feel like to be free,
To chase your dreams with wild abandon,
Knowing there's someone who cherishes your wings,
Lifting you higher, urging you to fly?

What would it feel like to be chosen,
Not for beauty alone, but for the depth of your mind,
Admired for the intricacies of your heart,
Seen as a unique soul, one of a kind?

What would it feel like to be safe,
In a home where love is warm and true,
Where a good meal and a glass of wine
Are shared without fear, no shadows lurking behind?

I've never known a love so deep,
So pure, so clear, so bright—
But if I could make just one wish,
I'd awaken to that love,
Before it slips away into the night.

PART 3: Me, Myself, & Wise

Introspection is the mirror...

"Mirror, mirror on the wall, who's the strongest of them all?" I ask, holding up the small reflective surface. I expect to see someone powerful, someone who has survived everything. But instead, the mirror reveals a tired face, worn down by battles I thought I had won.

"This can't be right," I mutter. "I've endured so much, fought so hard. I thought I'd see strength, not this weary version of myself."

The mirror seems to pause, then shifts, revealing a desolate landscape. "You did survive," it says softly, "but you're still carrying the weight of unseen wounds. What you see isn't just your face—it's the pain you haven't healed from. True strength comes from healing, and that takes time."

I take a deep breath, letting the truth settle in. The reflection stares back at me—a mixture of who I am now and who I'm striving to become. It's not what I expected, but perhaps it's exactly what I needed to see.

WHO AM I

When resistance is my armor,
And defiance, a whispered prayer,
I stand against the dark,
Believing I hold the flame,
Certain this power is mine.

But as I reach out,
Grasping at shadows,
Chasing illusions that slip away,
My grip falters—
The unknown, always out of reach.

I pursue fleeting pleasures,
Trying to fill the void with hollow triumphs,
Loneliness, a silent thief,
Whispers of empty escapes.

I avoid the mirror's stare,
Afraid of truths that unravel
The polished surface I've built.
Comfort lies in others' failures,
Judgment shields my heart,
But chaos follows,
Leaving only discontent.

Love buried beneath pride,
Hidden behind walls too high,
Becomes a distant echo,
A fragile memory fading.

Neglecting the body,
Choosing vanity over care,
I see despair in my reflection.
Clinging to half-truths for protection,
Wisdom slips from my grasp.

I hide behind passive aggression,
Calling it "boundaries," a shield.
Who am I when the mirror speaks?
When the mask cracks, and I dare to look?

In rare moments of quiet,
When noise fades, and pretense falls,
I glimpse the soul beneath the armor—
The strength I show, a cover for fear.

What happens when I lay down the sword?
When resistance yields to acceptance?
Can peace be found in embracing what is,
Instead of chasing what should be?
In that surrender, might I discover
The self I've hidden—whole,
Flawed, human, real?

There's a quiet yearning,
A voice speaking of vulnerability,
Of being enough without the mask.
In stillness, I wonder—
Could there be strength in letting go?
In allowing the light to find me,
Unafraid, unashamed,

Finally whole?

HEART, CONSUMED

Last night, I dreamt my heart was ripe fruit,
Dripping red, sweet as forgotten sins.
I fed pieces to the sky, hoping the stars
Would take my silence and leave me empty.

They gathered, laughing, mouths agape—
I opened my chest and watched the ocean spill.
Each wave carried a name, a memory washed away.
"Eat your heart out," they whispered,
And I did, with trembling hands.

They say, "You are what you consume."
But when I swallowed my heart,
I forgot my own name,
Forgot the pulse of who I was,
Replaced by what others demanded I be.

Wrapped in their gaze,
I offered the only thing that pulsed,
Leaving myself open, pages unread.
Their approval was all I craved,
Their shadows circled me like hungry wolves,
Drawn to the vulnerability I bled.

I followed the path they carved,
My choices shaped by their desires.
They say, "You are what you consume."
But when you consume only what others feed you,
What remains of the self?

I tore at my heart, soft as petals,
Blooming in reverse, each bite a question unanswered.
Their words curled like smoke in my throat,
Suffocating the voice I once owned.
I watched my heart crumble into dust,
Following the rhythm they set, not my own.

They say, "You are what you consume."
But when I tasted myself,
I realized I had never truly been whole,
Only a reflection of what they wanted to see.

Feast on what's left,
While I drown in wine as red as the sky,
Trying to forget the taste—
Tender, bittersweet, a life not lived.
My pulse fades, a slow rhythm unwound.

Who am I living for, with no heartbeat left of my own?
They say, "You are what you consume."
But when I swallowed my heart,
All that remained was silence—
The silence of a life led by others' hands,
Never my own.

UNCAGED SKY

Soft notes fall like tears from the sky,
Your voice, a distant echo I crave.
Red stains linger, wounds carved deep,
Whispers rise from a heart long caged.
Memories flicker in the shadows of time,
And wings, once clipped, yearn to fly.

Did you ever dream that you could fly?
Beneath the vast and limitless sky,
The years wore down the weight of time,
Yet still, your presence is what I crave.
Locked in the past, your spirit caged,
But strength endures in silence, deep.

The ache remains—it runs so deep,
Yet in the darkness, you still long to fly.
Once you lived a life so tightly caged,
Now you reach for the open sky,
Grasping the freedom that you crave,
Unraveling the tangled threads of time.

Shadows pull at the edges of time,
Tugging at scars buried far too deep.
In your quiet moments, it's peace you crave,
And though fear whispers, you may yet fly.
There's hope in the expanse of sky,
Even broken wings are no longer caged.

Once bound by sorrow, you were caged,

Lost within the endless maze of time.
But now there's light, a promise in the sky,
Guiding you through waters far too deep.
Now I see you, daring once more to fly,
Reaching for the healing that you crave.

A new song calls, a voice you crave,
No longer shackled, no longer caged.
You've found your wings, remembered how to fly,
Breaking free from the confines of time.
Your heart now sings, no longer buried deep,
The echoes of pain fade into the sky.

Yes, you will fly—no longer trapped by time,
No longer caged by wounds carved deep.
In the open sky, at last, you'll find what you crave.

SWING

Swing low, swing high—I hold two minds,
A storm gathers, pulling me in.
Torn between the ties that bind.

Each surge builds as calm unravels,
Lost in the pull of where I've been.
Swing low, swing high—I hold two minds.

Quiet fades, leaving little space
For peace to settle, to just begin.
Torn between the ties that bind.

I search for stillness, seek reprieve
From waves that toss me deep within.
Swing low, swing high—I hold two minds.

Can I escape what grips, confines,
That keeps me circling back again?
Torn between the ties that bind.

Balance slips further from my reach,
I rise, I fall, caught in the spin.
Swing low, swing high—I hold two minds,
Torn between the ties that bind.

BEAUTY

In the mirror, beauty is defined
By shapes and lines, by standards drawn—
Airbrushed skin, molded forms,
Chasing a norm I cannot conform to.

I spend hours on these fleeting dreams,
Choking on illusions, shrinking to feel whole.
Blaming the gaze that carves my silhouette,
Yet I keep running, consumed by the race.

"Why does sex sell?" I once asked.
"It's not for you," they laughed, so sure.
I've learned to offer what they crave,
A fleeting image on billboards.
He pays, I lose—
Still, I wonder why he feels entitled to take.

Wonders bought and sold,
In a world where beauty hides its face.
I twisted, bent, played the part,
But it's never enough—youth fades.

I'd pay any price to keep it close,
But it's all a trick, a billion-dollar snare,
Feeding on my fears, selling my pain.
Beauty, when controlled, loses its light,
Becoming a mirror of doubt.

But as I look closer, I begin to see—

All I wanted, all I needed,
Was to realize I never needed their lie.

Yet even now, the battle rages—
Knowing the truth but craving approval,
The mirror pulls me back, whispers promises—
"Just one more change, one more shift,
And maybe then you'll be enough."
I know I'm whole, yet the doubt creeps in,
A quiet voice that still holds power.

I should be free, yet I still chase
The ghost of perfection they planted inside.
I grasp at this reflection, trying to believe—
Trying to love what I know is already mine.
But the struggle lingers, the need to conform
Fades slowly, like smoke in the light.
I am whole, I know it now,
But some days, it's harder to feel than to say.

WHAT IS THIS SKIN

What is this skin I inhabit?
Once, the question suffocated me—
Shame coiled tight like chains,
The weight of flesh and color heavy on my soul.
Yet strength and honor—gifts of Earth and Mother—
Lay buried beneath a colonized history,
Truth trampled under the feet
Of those who came before.

Their struggles, their blood—
Not the sum of who they were,
But the force that made them stronger.
History—woven by victors,
A suit of false armor,
Stripping truth until it choked.

In my reflection, I saw a nation's shame,
Forgot to see the beauty within the pain,
Neglected to stand tall for those
Who sacrificed so I could dream
Of who I might become—because I am free.

Separation is death.
A culture distorted,
A heritage commodified,
A people exploited.

Yet facing the trauma, hearing the song my body sings—
Echoes of mothers, daughters, sisters, sons—

I found strength to rise,
For therein lies power.

Now I see, I hear, I embrace
The rhythm of my skin, my hair—
The beauty inherent in me.
Born of Black strength,
I was made to stand tall—
Not to prove, but to understand,
To honor my roots.

So, what is this skin?
It is but skin,
Not the sum of who I am,
But a reminder I am more.
A hue of warmth,
A testament to strength and honor,
From a proud people of warriors.
What is this?
It is my skin.

DICHOTOMY OF SELF

I gaze upon myself,
Suspended between restraint and wildness,
As if modesty could stifle
The stirrings beneath my skin.
Is it wrong to yearn for rebellion,
To defy the expectations others impose,
And pursue the desires that call to me?

Who am I in this unrelenting tug-of-war?
If I am forever self-conscious, can I ever be free?
Self-discovery is like sifting through soil,
Hands plunged deep, raw and unclean.
There is fear in confronting oneself,
In facing the flawed, yet radiant truth.

Turning away from the mirror only deepens confusion,
Leaving you wandering, uncertain of your place.
A perfect reflection can be blinding,
Like a smile concealing what lies beneath.
Yet truth is delicate—
Like breath on glass, it fades swiftly,
Easily overlooked.
Living for applause,
You dread the quiet moments,
Fearing what they might reveal.
But growth is found amid the thorns,
A rose blooming after the struggle.
The path is never linear—
It winds and strays,

And in moments of doubt, where you feel lost,
That is where your roots take hold.

I stand before myself,
Both restrained and untamed.
So who am I, truly?
Perhaps the answer lies within the journey itself,
In the questions I ask, the steps I take.

Balance emerges through confronting myself,
No matter how difficult it may be.
Perhaps perfection lies in embracing the wild,
In all its messy, beautiful chaos.
It takes courage to delve deep,
To uncover who I truly am.
Balance is not about choosing a side—
It is about embracing both,
Understanding that the journey never truly ends.

I WONDER

I sit between two worlds,
A question balanced in each hand.
Self-doubt wraps itself around me—what is truth?
I've wandered so long, I now wonder:
Which path do I take?

One voice in one hand spins,
"Eternity is a black hole—
Why search for answers when they lead to more questions?
Truth is fluid, a reflection of your will.
If life is a gift, why should there be struggle?
Master your desires, grasp at power,
Chase riches, control what you can.
Discipline breeds strength; the weak will falter.
The game is yours if you're ruthless enough to play."

What is truth?
What is mine?
Do I even know what holds meaning?
Is truth a construct, a veil I lift or wear?
So many roads unfurl before me.
I wonder.
The other voice, softer, whispers,
"One truth guides you inward,
Not to entangle, but to focus.
Wisdom brings clarity—
One path to follow, one destination awaits.
Miracles blossom in stillness,
Strife is often a consequence of choice.

Free will shapes us, and others' choices leave their mark,
But grace, when embraced, offers peace.
Storms can uproot, but the strongest trees bend, not break.
Life isn't without trials, but nothing worthy is."

Yet one truth feels constricting,
A single path seems narrow, limiting.
I believe this, or I believe that—
New ideas bloom, and with them, my mind shifts.
Can I truly rise, live fully,
While walking a linear road? I wonder.

So, which do I choose?
Self-actualization across many paths,
Or one truth that transcends fleeting desires?
Knowledge for power never satisfies,
A hunger always reaching for more.
But wisdom, rooted in stillness, brings peace.
Is the search for meaning endless,
Or is surrender where freedom lies?
Each path demands a price—
Do I chase every desire,
Crafting my truth from fleeting whims,
Or trust in a greater order, beyond my understanding?

Could I rest in one truth,
Knowing I'm not alone,
That perfection is not required?
One voice roars, bold and certain,
The other whispers softly, inviting me in.
What is truth, I wonder—one truth or many?
In the asking, I begin the journey,

Each step a question, each answer a path.
I take a step—uncertain, yet still I wonder.

GRAPPLINE FAITH

What is faith?
I've never trusted blindly.
I control what I can.
"Control what you can control," they say,
Because life is too fragile to leave to chance.

Yet there's irony in that—
I believe in a universe vast beyond comprehension,
In gravity, a force unseen yet real,
But faith in something else unseen,
A whisper in the quiet,
An echo in the dark—
Still, I hesitate.

Isn't it strange?
I trust in futures I cannot predict,
In possibilities not yet real,
Yet stumble over the idea of a presence
Equally elusive, equally unknown.

If I surrender control,
Do I lose power, autonomy?
Perhaps I like the illusion of control.
But in the silence,
When I sit with my thoughts,
I stare at the sky,
Hoping for something beyond this,
Hoping that there's more than what I see.

I sought a good life—
I worked for it, dreamed of it.
So why isn't it enough?
Because...
All along, I feared I'd be found lacking,
Worried they'd see me as a fraud.
So I hustled, cheated,
Manifested the life I wanted.
But even when it came to pass,
The emptiness remained.

I control my path,
Yet deep down, I know I'm lost.
Everything I hold could vanish in an instant.
So perhaps I could have faith in something unseen.
Maybe it's not a lack of faith—
Perhaps it's fear of the truth:
I cannot bend the universe to my will.
I'm running in circles,
So maybe faith in a God of the infinite
Is the grace I've been denying.
Maybe faith isn't relinquishing control—
It's learning I don't have to carry it all alone.
Maybe it's the voice that speaks after the storm,
Telling me that even in the vast unknown,
I'm never truly alone.

I couldn't leave life to chance,
But maybe He offers something lasting,
Something that doesn't imprison, but frees.
Faith isn't easy, even when I say I'll trust.
Life has left me swimming,

My trust bent, shattered, abandoned.
I can't seem to trust anyone to stay,
But maybe, if I open my heart,
If I trust in God—
Maybe I'll learn that I don't need to fear.

GRACE UNEARNED

Once, I believed we could live without regret—
Diamond and ruby, rare and bright,
A bond so precious we held it close.
But dazzled by our brilliance,
I let him tear us apart,
Petals scattered on the wind, too light to hold.

Did he see our rarity, or was that the allure?
Did he crave us more because of it?
A cerulean wink, a grin igniting fire in the dark—
He danced between us, unseen,
A hunter stalking the night.

I watched him promise you endless summers,
Only to see them fade,
Like the shimmer of a dream slipping away.
When his eyes met mine,
I should've turned, hidden my care,
But I was caught—
The thrill of the forbidden, a secret I couldn't keep.

In my betrayal, your trust shattered like glass.
Solitude became my silent burden,
Need, a sin I couldn't shake.
Attraction, a gleaming armor that weighed me down,
A desire that refused to dim.
I craved the gaze that validated,
As if it could fill the void,
As if I was owed what had been denied.

All the while, the storm inside churned,
Thunder of envy, a tornado swirling beneath.
I never understood how fragile we were,
That even the strongest bonds can fall like stars.
It didn't have to be him, though it was—
The choice I made cut deeper than the act,
Revealing a need I could no longer hide.

A shadow veiled my truest self,
Brokenness poisoning my soul.
To rebuild what's lost is a steep climb,
Longer than the bond we once forged—
A summit we may never reach.

Yet from the dust, something might rise,
Forged with care beneath clearer skies.
Not all can be remade, but it takes two
To tend the fragile threads of what's shared.
Forgiveness—a path slow and hard,
Far more difficult than letting go.

It's a choice, day by day,
To move beyond the hurt and the fray.
I could've been left in the cold,
Shut out from the warmth we knew,
But you blessed me with one more dance—
A waltz between friends, fragile yet true.

Where rust could have claimed our memory,
You gave the unearned gift of another chance.
In quiet moments, we heal

What time alone could never erase.

SIX WAS MAGIC

We rolled three pairs into one,
Laughter echoing, endless fun.
Siblings gliding down familiar streets,
Six lives intertwined where joy would meet.

A blend of sweetness, pure and true—
Once, we knew the magic of six.
We chased the sun, radiant and bright,
Carved our world from morning till night.

Tight as a tapestry, woven strong,
A bond we believed would last lifelong.
But time, the thief, moved swift and sly,
And slowly, new paths pulled us awry.

Now nostalgia lingers bittersweet,
Echoes of laughter with each fading beat.
We were stars, close and clear,
Now scattered, distant—some here, some nowhere.

Where did the stone fall that fractured us?
When did the cracks begin to show?
In the yard where dreams once soared,
We stood strong, side by side—
Now I wonder, was it all just a fleeting memory?

Sides were taken, edges grew sharp,
Time cut deep, despite our hearts.
Can we find our way back to when six was magic,

Unbroken, whole, as it was back then?
As the years passed and tides turned,
Still my heart aches, still it yearns.
Wounds unhealed, words unheard,
A house forsaken, a home spurned.

Where does that leave us now?
How do we bridge the chasm, heal the rift?
Where love's walls once stood firm,
Can we rebuild on the same sacred ground?

At an altar of patience and grace,
Where sharp edges soften, and time finds its place,
Can we reclaim the magic of six once more,
And reignite the warmth that once held us tight?

I JUST NEED

I just need—
Though I'm not sure what that means.
Quiet, perhaps?
The noise unsettles,
Pulls me from where I'm meant to be.

What I need is silence.
I crave a moment to plunge deep—
This is my process;
My art requires air,
But what I need, they never concede.

On the page, I take on many forms.
I'm the seductress,
Tracing the raw ache of longing.
What I need is a space of stillness,
One just for me.

I could scream—
I do scream.
My mind pulses with a migraine's sting,
Yet still, you ask for my time.
Like Woolf and Plath,
I tread a solitary path.

What I need is sanctuary,
A reflection in deep waters—just me.
At night, the ceiling becomes a map of stars.
Darkness isn't a threat; it's a guide,

Revealing what the day hides,
Quiet truths cast by night.

I long for quiet,
To feel my skin rise
In moments when words drift on the breeze.
In silence, my thoughts find release.
I need the quiet,
I need to hear myself.
In the woods, I follow the silence,
Letting my thoughts roar.
Embracing stillness,
In the quest for more.

In the hush,
I reclaim pieces of my soul, once lost,
Gathering them in the dark,
At any cost.

THE JOURNAL

Sometimes, words arrive effortlessly—
They slip onto the page, warm in my hands,
A connection to something beyond,
A quiet pulse where thoughts take shape—
Natural, instinctive, true.

In the still hours, the muse finds me,
And together we move, wordless,
A rhythm in the night.
Letters carry my secrets,
Emotions entangled within the lines.
I am the wind's distant echo,
The soft patter of rain on deserted streets.

Inspiration surges like headlights on an empty road,
Lifting me high, only to set me down
In the restless flow of creation.
I am the dancer—focused, driven.
This is not merely desire; it's a summons.
Onstage, I shed my masks, searching
For the girl who hides behind shame.

Once, lies shielded me—fragile, yet safe,
Balancing truth with illusion.
But now, I live differently—
In a reality reshaped, part fact, part dream.
I weave romance and mystery,
Blending imagination with fragments of history.

Words unravel me, even as they bind me whole.
My words carry desire, ever reaching,
Pushing forward.
They build, sharp when needed,
Cutting deep, leaving indelible marks.
I am both gentle and fierce—
This is me, in every line.

With words comes responsibility.
When wielded wisely, they open windows,
And in the silence, stories take shape,
Offering paths forward.
This is more than fiction, more than a pastime—
It is the art of living,
Breathing life into all I am,
And all I strive to be.
It's more than words—
It is a journey, a reckoning,
A truth unfolding.

REFLECTION

"Do you see me?"
"I see you."
"When I turn away, do you still?"
"Yes, I do."
"What do you see when you gaze back at me?"
"I see beauty; your smile ripples the dance of flames."

"Where does your gaze wander when it shifts?"
"I wonder if the reflection changes."
"Why?"
"Because I fear losing sight of you."
"Of me?"
"Yes—who am I without you?"
"You are me, and I am you—always."

"Yet sometimes, you avert your eyes,
As if searching for something hidden within the cracks of the glass."
"Sometimes, I despise my own reflection."
"Why?"
"I'm not sure. Maybe I've forgotten who I am."

"Look at me."
"Why?"
"Because you are still beautiful—like planets in orbit,
Bursting with light.
You've forgotten how to see yourself, to see us.
When you remember, you'll know—
For you are me, and we are a life, bright and full."

ROSE COLORED SKY

A rose-colored sky,
The sun warm upon our skin.
Summer stretched endlessly, as if youth would never fade.
We sang *The Reason*, our voices perfectly in sync—
It was our anthem, our world to shape.

"So why worry?"—that was our dare,
To take flight, to soar, no fear in the air.
We lived on desire, caffeine, and time,
Partied all night beneath strings of lights,
Our star burning bright—the boys couldn't look away.

Wind wild in our hair,
Road trips in the Jetta—
Did we know where we were headed?
We didn't care.
Arms raised high,

Our stories became dares, lyrics written across the sky.
Warm sand beneath our feet,
Where waves met our secrets, sinking deep.
Like starfish, we had dreams, we had wishes—
You never live more fully than at eighteen.

Back when our bracelets jingled in rhythm,
Before life was uploaded, hashtagged, defined.
When desire was a wick burning bright,
And everyone wanted to be us, wanted to shine.

Together, we were more—
Not just best friends, we were something transcendent.
Friendship felt real in those quiet nights,
When we shared our fears, wept in the dark.

Perched on car hoods, sneaking sips of beer,
No worries, no cares, just dancing beneath the stars.
We found ourselves in the churn of the tide,
In every dip, every turn,
Burning brighter, we lit up our world.

Maybe, one day, we could stop time,
And return to that world beneath a rose-colored sky.

JOY

I laugh—
My smile, playful and unrestrained, lights the room.
I see it now, frozen in time:
A witty remark, a sharp retort,
Those moments when the world felt like mine.

Feet light as air, spinning in ecstasy,
Laughter cascading into tears,
Spirits high, popcorn in hand,
A film flickering in the comforting darkness.

A six-way embrace, arms intricately entwined—
We sat on the shore, sharing stories,
The briny scent of sea salt thick in the air,
A blanket of familial warmth wrapped around us.

Our smiles illuminated the night as the bonfire crackled,
Gathered beneath a sky strewn with vigilant stars.
I still feel the sand beneath my toes,
The fire's glow blending with the cool breath of the sea.

Flirtatious quips, swift and sharp—
Laughter rang through the night like music,
Fingers dancing over screens, texts sent in a blur.
Late-night indulgence with wild friends,
Another evening of reckless joy.

Heading home with food in hand,
We were a tribe, bound by shared adventure.

The salty fries, the sweet soda—
A taste of nights when we felt invincible.

Surrounded by my people—
Those who loved and fiercely guarded me,
We radiated energy, sparks crackling like fire.
Such rare kinship—they saw me, truly saw me.
I always knew they had my back.

Hand in hand, we faced the world,
The adventures that became our most cherished tales.
Even now, when life grows heavy,
I draw strength from those memories,
Knowing we stood together.

Back then, tomorrow's worries were distant, unreal.
If I had to distill it all,
Those moments were my truest joy.

HOLD ME/THE FUTURE US

Sometimes, I simply need you to hold me,
Let the tears fall as they may—just stay near.
When I ascend too high, tether me with care,
Intuit the moments I long for tenderness,
Or sense the need for silence, a sanctuary of space.

Dance with me beneath the velvet summer sky,
Feel when laughter mends my soul.
Know when the lightest touch will suffice,
Hold me close as I unravel,
Raise me like a pillar—steadfast, unyielding.

I ask only that you steady me,
Be the one I trust, unwavering.
When I rush ahead, consumed,
Be the anchor that paces my stride,
A love constant and sure.

Together, we'll sway, cradled by the night,
A kiss so gentle, yet rich in meaning.
Though I am a whirlwind, rising and falling,
All I ask is for you to remain, resolute.
I seek strength, for I am strong—
Strong enough to stand, yet needing you
To shield me from myself when I falter.

I promise a life brimming with fullness,
To love you through frost, to love you through flame.
Sometimes, I simply need you to hold me,

And in that moment, I will unveil to you
A world of wonders, dreams whispered.

I can be anything—but with you,
I will be more.

PART 4: Finding Flight

Without hope, peace loses its purpose...

To gaze at the horizon is a blessing—a promise of light beyond the dark woods, where the path remains uncertain. I've felt the weight of the long journey, energy drained to the last drop. Yet, just when I believed I couldn't take another step, I found that I could.

Peace arrived quietly, almost imperceptibly. At first, it was frustrating—peace isn't something you can seize or demand. I've searched for easy answers, especially when life's climb felt steep.

I've watched others from a distance, their lives seemingly perfect—cruising on vacations, dressed in dreams, driving nice cars, surrounded by beauty. It seemed they had everything I longed for.

But I've realized that what shines from afar often reveals itself as hollow, fleeting. The polished glow of gold dulls quicker than expected. I reached for joy in places I thought it would reside, only to find it vanish as quickly as it appeared. Yet, when I chose to continue down the road less traveled—my own road—I began to unearth treasures that truly endure.

An easy life may be tempting, but it's fleeting, like sand slipping through fingers. A life filled with purpose? That's where the real gold lies. In that purpose, I've learned to rise above the world's distractions. I've found peace—not in what the world offers, but in the quiet strength of a journey well-chosen.

HITTING BOTTOM

Wrapped in smoke, I choke on night's breath,
Falling swiftly through star-sewn seams—no light there.
Control slips like sand from empty hands,
Worry roots in a garden unraveling.
Where I once walked on clouds of green,
The earth yawns wide, swallowing everything.

Rock bottom—who knew it came with wings?
Sunlight splinters through webs of thought,
Clouds thickening like whispers long forgotten.
What was solid now drifts to air,
Like petals frozen mid-breath.
From this low, I call in vain—
Echoes twist like coiling rain.

Rock bottom—how did I fall into this dream?
Shadows crawl through time's cracked seams,
Where life once thrived, now it unwinds.
Had I cried louder to the wind,
Would roses bloom where ghosts now bend?
If I'd been wiser, would I have seen
The loss of what was once so green?

Rock bottom—it's a garden I never meant to tend.
Worry storms, thunder hums far off,
Where roses bloomed, sorrow now drops.
Each door I turn reflects a lie,
Paths vanish like whispers on the breeze.
Could I have saved the curled-up blooms,

Where shadows danced and sorrow loomed?
Rock bottom—who knew I'd glow so low?

But listen—whispers stir the dust:
Rock bottom's not a fall, but trust.
Look up—the sky bends, stars spill down,
Filling cracks where dreams had drowned.
The sky, an ocean, waves climbing high—
Stars, seeds waiting to break and fly.
What are stars but blooms untamed,
Lighting paths through worlds unnamed?

A gift unasked, yet here just the same.
After storms have torn it through,
Life bursts where the old withdrew.
Live not the life that fades away,
But one where roots grip firm and stay.
Walk on air with soles remade,
Carved from lessons that never fade.
Losing all you thought you knew,
A garden's soul will bloom anew.

A storm's not an end, but wind that clears
The earth so hope can reappear.
Sometimes, the old must crumble to dust,
For new wings to rise from rust.
Revived, reborn, the leaves now sing—
Of chaos, grace, and life's wild wings.

LOST IN THE JUNGLE

Vines tighten, pulling me deep into night,
The ground slipping beneath my feet, no path clear.
Shadows coil around, whispering fear,
Rainstorms rise, drowning all hope in silence.
I pray for a Guide to lead me from despair,
But the jungle thickens, binding me to the dark.

Predators flicker at the edge of the dark,
Their eyes reflecting the endless night.
In each breath, I feel the weight of despair—
No light pierces through, no answers seem clear.
I call out, but the sky returns only silence,
And the vines twist tighter, feeding my fear.

I stumble forward, my steps heavy with fear,
Lost in this wilderness, swallowed by dark.
The cries of the jungle echo through silence,
Filling my chest with the cold of night.
Each step feels endless, though no path is clear,
And with each turn, I sink deeper into despair.

What is hope in a place woven from despair?
Where the trees breathe doubt, and the air breeds fear?
The paths I once knew fade, nothing is clear,
And I wonder if I'll ever escape this dark.
The jungle thrives on the endlessness of night,
Smothering my voice until there's only silence.

Yet from the depths of this thickening silence,

A whisper stirs, parting the veil of despair.
It tells me I wasn't meant to walk alone in night—
That I need not surrender to my deepest fear.
In the distance, faint but steady in the dark,
A shimmer of light begins to cut through, clear.

The Guide appears, their presence calm and clear,
A voice like starlight, unraveling the silence.
They reach for me, a beacon in the dark,
Reminding me I can rise from despair.
No longer bound by the vines of fear,
I step forward, following them out of night.

Through the night, the path is finally clear—
Fear dissolves into silence, no longer despair.
The Guide leads, starlight soft and sure through the dark.

UNBOUND

You stared me down, shadow heavy above,
Fear creeping in—I dropped my gaze, chilled.
You thought you could crush me beneath your weight,
Pressed harder, savoring my stumble,
Gleeful as cracks widened,
Your disdain coiling around me like smoke,
Choking the breath from my lungs.

Tears, sweat, soil—mud pulling me deeper,
Each step, a struggle.
You stood tall, laughter cold,
As I hung my head in shame—
Your words, debris on the wind,
A stench like rot,
Seeping into the fractures of my soul.

You tried to blind me with false shimmer,
And I fell, dismissing His hand in my shame.
You laughed as I refused to be saved,
Clawing alone at the embankment,
The whisper of mercy drowned in your scorn.
But what you didn't see—what I forgot—
Was the spark, dimmed but never gone,
A light you tried to smother, still pulsing deep,
Waiting, biding time.

You hated me for that light—
For what I was, for what I could become,
Because I had already been saved,

And you needed me to forget.
The waters rose, my tears flooding the earth,
And when I could no longer stand,
I remembered the hand once offered,
Crying out—"Please, I can't do this anymore."

Strength lifted me from the deep,
Unexpected, placing me on solid ground.
Warm hands pressed against my chest,
And the water I swallowed poured out.
I looked up, breathless—
Love, felt by my heart alone.
Shivering in the cold, it surged within me,
A fire, growing deep inside.

That light flared, fed by anger and truth.
Empowered, flames in my eyes, I turned to you—
The one who loomed over me,
Now crouched in the shadows, wounded.
You knew I wasn't blind anymore,
And I would not forget.

My anger rose—fueled by something greater,
Stronger than yours.
I met your gaze, head-on.
Who are you to make me small?
Who are you to strip my power?
Once a beautiful angel—now just a shadow.
You thought you were greater—
Than the Creator we both bow to.

You fell, not I—it was never my weight to carry.

Only a coward holds another captive
For their failure.
With grace, He paid your ransom—
Your burden is no longer mine.

He returned me to life, and that's why
You fought to make me forget—
But I won't.
Now I stand, staring you down,
No longer bowed, no longer broken.
I see you.
Run back to your shadows—
I am unbound.

ME

I am the quiet sum of dreams,
Whispers flickering, soft yet sure.
I've learned to cradle my own light,
Letting it rise and fall like breath unbidden.
Life veered from the script I once envisioned,
Yet I climbed steep hills with trembling hands.
Though storms raged, I no longer cower—
I am not the weight of chains that once bound me.

If happiness is a journey, it begins here,
With each step taken in the darkest hour,
Chasing shadows, stumbling through memories,
Fingers raw, reaching for the light.
I was lost in the stillness of despair,
My heart tangled in threadbare hope—
Then came a pause—
A breath before dawn whispered gently,
And in that quiet, I found the spark,
A flame patiently waiting within.

I no longer bury myself beneath the past's weight.
I am not broken; I am becoming,
A patchwork of scars and dreams,
Stitched together by strength earned.
No more hiding.
I rise, unravel, and bloom.

Now, when I look ahead,
I see not just battles survived,

But the path unfurling before me,
Each step lit by the light I've carried all along.
The future is no longer a question,
But a promise—woven from my becoming.
I am not merely the sum of my past—I am more.
I have always belonged.
And here, in this moment, I am free.

END, START

I sigh against shattered glass, tracing a heart,
What I once mistook for a ghostly breath.
Where I end, You start.

Lost in the dark, torn apart,
Your flame rose steady, guarding me from death.
I sigh against shattered glass, tracing a heart.

Through thickening shadows, You played Your part,
Guiding me softly with each quiet breath.
Where I end, You start.

In chaos deep, with all my fragile parts,
Your glow pulled me gently from beneath.
I sigh against shattered glass, tracing a heart.

As I fall, You catch with art,
Mending cracks with grace and depth.
Where I end, You start.

What I resisted from the very start
Led me here, to a place of greater breadth.
I sigh against shattered glass, tracing a heart—
Where I end, You start.

THE MISSED MEANINGS

I cried for miracles, blind to signs,
Missing blessings drifting by like whispers.
In chasing wonders, I lost their meaning—
Miracles don't always arrive as dreams,
But they come in perfect time.

Thirsting for floods to quench my soul,
I overlooked the soft rain weaving through.
Crying for miracles, blind to signs—
I missed the sip I needed, gentle and true,
Much easier to drink.

In winds of frustration, wisdom fades,
While truth waits in silence, quietly grieving.
Chasing grand signs, I lost the meaning—
Little moments glimmer softly,
Until they grow and gleam.

When hard times rose, clouding my view,
I forgot the grace He placed in me.
Crying for miracles, blind to signs—
I missed the strength He forged within.
I grow by practicing.

I missed the signs He softly reveals,
Daily miracles, quietly received.
Chasing fears, I lost the meaning:
It's darkest just before the light,
But dawn will rise again.

In quiet grace, strength unfurls like morning light.
"Trust me," He whispers, "it's alright."
Once crying for miracles, blind to signs,
Chasing my own understanding,
I lost the meaning—
His wonders surround me.

SHOW ME

Teach me,
Like streams winding through forests,
Water bending around roots and stones.
Guide me,
As I walk this path,
Listening for the pulse beneath the earth,
The current waiting to carry me.

I once wandered without direction,
Pouring my heart into thirsty ground,
Chasing trails that led nowhere,
Spilling into someone else's stream.

Show me
How to live like water through stone—
Quiet, steady, reflecting light.
Not a fleeting mist at dawn,
But a deep well, full and enduring.

Help me find love that stays,
Like rain soaking forgotten soil,
Where even shadows reach for its touch.

Lead me
With the quiet strength of rivers carving canyons,
Patient, unstoppable, shaping the unseen.
Hold me
In a meadow where wildflowers bend,
Their stems leaning toward the wind

That whispers Your name.

Teach me
To hear the song of still waters,
The slow drip of life beneath the surface.
To find the rhythm of trees drinking from hidden springs,
And the peace of being carried
By a stream that knows its way.

Though I've grown,
I return to the Source,
Kneeling by the spring, hands open,
Listening for the hum of water against stone.

Perhaps I lacked the map to follow,
To know how water heals—
Not through motion alone,
But in its quiet depth.

So now I ask,
Show me Your Spirit within,
The rivers etched into my bones.
Reveal who I am becoming,
Like water shaping the world in silence—
Soft, steady,
Quietly unstoppable.

ELASTIC HEART

I was soft,
A blank slate waiting for life to shape me.
"I am naïve," I whispered to the sky,
And the clouds carried my words away.
"I am unwise," I thought,
As the moon stood still—
Silent, steady,
Turning through the night.

My heart felt as though it flowed backward,
Caught between the past and present.
Fragile, yet resilient,
It stretched to hold more than I could bear,
Reaching for light always just out of reach.

But even the strongest hearts can break,
Pulled too tightly by unseen forces.
Still, they heal—
Not through sheer strength, but by softening,
Finding light within the cracks.
Each scar, a marker,
A testament to what I endured.

Every tear showed a new direction,
And in the ruins, I discovered seeds of something new.
"How did you endure?" they ask,
But they didn't see how I bent,
Reshaped by time and struggle.

With each challenge, I stretched further,
My heart growing stronger,
Yet never losing its softness.
The universe moved with me,
And I—still kind, still open—
Rose from the depths, unbroken.

Now I stand,
My heart wide,
Each scar a testament,
Each tear a guide.
Shaped by trials, stretched and tested,
But always reborn—
A heart that holds its strength within,
Unyielding, yet gentle.

GRIEVE

Today, I weep—
For shadows that linger,
For echoes of a self long lost.
Worn and weary, my spirit heavy,
I seek solace in the stillness.
But wait—a voice whispers:
"Grief," it says, "is a bridge."
"A bridge?" I ask.
"Yes, a passage to the heart's hidden places.
You grieve for shame, for burdens past,
For what was clear, and the blindness you called sight.
Yet within this sorrow, light can be found."

Embrace the grace within the ache,
For what I offer is beyond understanding.
I will carry your weight, lift you higher,
Turn your fears into stars to guide you.
Restore what was lost, bless it twice over—
For every tear shed, a deeper joy awaits.
As you walk through shadows,
Feeling the pull of descent,
I am the soft light at the summit, calling.

The Spirit waits with quiet patience,
My Son walks beside you,
Ready for the moment you reach out,
So He can lead you home.
From ashes and scars,
We call for your return,

To guide you from sorrow's depths,
To heal the burn.

So weep, release, let go—
Grief is the door.
Through it, peace enters,
And the weight you carried
Is no longer yours.

BIRTH

What is birth?
My body stretched like the horizon, cracking open, spilling stars—
I loathed the galaxies I was made to carry.
You sprouted inside me, a flower with iron roots,
Twisting me into unfamiliar landscapes.
They called it beauty. I called it something else—
A parasite drawing light from my bones.
I was diminished, a fading constellation.

In the quiet, cloaked in soft misery,
Did I wish for you?
Or did you pull me from the void,
Unmistakable in your choice to be mine?
Why don't I feel what they say I should?
You kicked—I felt the tremors,
My thoughts unraveling into dust,
Expanding, a universe swallowing itself whole.

Dreams vivid, unfamiliar aches,
Glimpses of stars colliding in other realms.
Still, I drift between what was and what will be—
Incomplete, yet whole.
The world spins, and I spin with it.
I sigh as hands reach to touch me,
You kick, anchoring me to a ground I no longer recognize.

Who will you be?
Will you mirror me, like a reflection in a fractured sky?
Will you even like me?

Can one ask such questions of the universe?
It makes you question everything.
Am I a vessel, carved from stars, bearing life?
Or a universe unto myself, boundless and expanding?

Does it matter? Do we matter?
Are we merely clusters of atoms, drifting in the void?
There is no true end, no beginning.
The universe folds in on itself.
And I drift.
Perhaps when you arrive, you'll tell me who we are.

What journey have you taken,
You, who raced into existence like lightning through clouds?
What lies beyond the enchantment that formed you?
So I pushed.
The sky broke apart—
I breathed, and stars fell like rain.
I breathed again. I pushed through the light.
I breathed, and the universe gasped.

When you crossed the threshold, I wondered—
What life will you find in the ashes of stars?
For me, engulfed in fire, I thought I might perish.
What is birth?
It is the universe, ever-expanding,
Tearing itself apart to create you.
I formed life within me.
You took shape from heaven's glow.

Now you are here, and I—
I have been reborn,

And I am no longer the same.

AURA

I dive deep into the sea's calm embrace,
Descending into unknown depths,
Relinquishing everything—fear dissolves.
For without You, nothing holds meaning.
Love, without You, remains shallow, still.

We wander through ancient groves,
Playing hide and seek in quiet moments
Where Your spirit lingers, ever-present.
You take my hand, leading me forward,
Light unfolding Your aura—
A gift promising endless tomorrows.

You unveil freedom beyond the world's cages.
In a field where fireflies dance,
Their light kisses twilight,
And I stand, filled with wonder and trust.
Your gaze pierces my soul,
Within it, hope stirs, new possibilities arise,
As the world gently settles into night.

I float above, wrapped in Your light,
Just out of reach, in the games we play.
You teach me the sacred dance—
Not to capture my heart, but to fortify it.
Guiding me through a world of mystery,
Revealing my own light, showing me faith.

We stand together, You and I,

Watching time's melodies drift by.
I cannot see the hidden currents,
Yet You show me how to soar,
Turning the world into wonder,
Revealing beauty in the unseen,
Unlocking the stars' secrets,
Sharing the universe's forgotten song.

LOVE

Love blooms softly, light rising from the soul,
Given freely, it radiates, it glows.
Love isn't meant to be held—it's meant to unfold.

Locked inside, it cannot make us whole;
It withers in silence where kindness doesn't flow.
Love blooms softly, light rising from the soul.

When offered, love smolders, a steady coal,
A warmth that deepens, soft and slow.
Love isn't meant to be held—it's meant to unfold.

I'll love you fiercely, where hearts unroll;
With every touch, our connection grows.
Love blooms softly, light rising from the soul.

Our love, a truth we carve from what we hold—
I heal you with hands that life bestows.
Love isn't meant to be held—it's meant to unfold.

In love's still glow, both tender and bold,
Together, we find where its wisdom shows.
Love blooms gently, like light from the soul—
Love isn't mine to keep—it's meant to unfold.

VISION

In true love, there are no bounds, no vows.
It plunges deep, retreats like waves,
Soars where sky meets earth,
Music unheard, dancing through time—
A vision fleeting—here, then gone.
Dreamers never rest until they find
A love that sets them apart, undefined.

They see beyond stories, believe in the unseen,
Knowing the cost to keep love serene,
Chasing music felt but never heard,
In realms where dreams are born.
At birth, we forget, yet still we ache
For a place where love grows stronger,
Where visions of light never break.

We search for what's lost inside,
Yearning for solace, striving to abide,
Longing for melodies from ages unknown,
In visions honed by light, quietly shown.
These notes unfurl, a symphony unheard—
Strings and crescendos through worlds interred.

What is Heaven but galaxies entwined?
Why choose the real when dreams unwind?
To hear the music that echoes through time,
In realms where the unreal blooms.

A tale of history—some are lies,

Yet stories of love still soothe as we sleep.
Why stifle the dreams we long to keep,
Seeking music from eons past,
Embracing the unreal, where visions grow vast?

I yearn for a love that lifts me high,
Reviving the dreamer where dreams once lay.
To be consumed, immersed in light,
Releasing old wounds, shedding their blight.
I seek a melody, timeless and free,
To dance in ethereal realms—
The Composer and me.

MY BOUNDLESS LIGHT

In your tiny hands, a universe unfolds—
Stars spark in your eyes, galaxies twirl at your touch.
You light the room, a beacon in the dark,
Your laughter—a melody that chases shadows away.
In your giggles, my heart finds its rhythm,
Dancing to the music of your joy.

As you drift into dreams, I stand watch,
Whispering prayers like a soft breeze—
For health, for strength, for joy,
For a future boundless as the sky.
You are the gift I never knew I needed,
A light that illuminates my soul.

In your gaze, a silent question—
A search for answers I cannot always give.
But sometimes, the truth in our hearts
Is the only answer we need.
I long to see you soar, to help you find your wings,
To watch you grow into who you're meant to be.

When you build your castles of blocks,
Fingers tracing ancient stories in the soil,
I marvel at the wonder in your eyes—
The world, already a canvas, vivid and wide.
Even in your quiet, your story unfolds,
A tale of greatness written deep in your soul.

From your first cry to our first embrace,

You've shown me a light I didn't know I sought.
I will stand beside you, move mountains if I must,
To see you rise, to remind you—
No love could be greater than mine.

May you find connection with the divine,
A life prayed for, covered in grace.
You've expanded my heart, transformed its space—
My son,
You are the universe, boundless and bright.

WHAT WAS IT WORTH

What was it worth in the end, to me?
It was worth everything—a truth I now see.
What is life without the ache of suffering?
My scars, born from fire, shaped who I am.
In each burn, I found depth—not in daylight's shallow glow,
But where my essence rooted deep in the dark.
I slipped through the rabbit hole, nights unraveling me,
And from those depths, I forged the steel of my soul.
Each wound, a tempered blade, slicing through shadow,
Until dawn bled light—no longer a pawn, I rose.

What remains when we deny the struggles that shape us?
Missed whispers of dreams, cast adrift in the void.
Wisdom blooms in strife's dark soil.
Down, down I fell, seeking healing oil.
My words tangled, thorns in their haste,
Yet every thorn bore sweetness, lessons in disguise.
In the mirror, I searched my core,
Through the rabbit hole, yearning for more.

What is the worth of stripping bare the soul?
To peel back every layer, exposing hidden shades,
To uncover what shines when light is scarce.
Through the depths, I plunged, seeking the truth of me.
Had I only walked where the sun bathed me whole,
I'd have missed the wisdom whispered in the shadows,
The quiet strength found only in night's embrace.
I needed that darkness—its veil sharpened my sight.
Through the rabbit hole, I sought insight's edge.

What was it worth when all was done?
It was worth everything—the battles I've won,
Each scar a line etched deep in my song.

RUN

Shadows stretch, lengthening your stride.
When the storm shatters silence, fear tightens its grip—
But listen—
A whisper stirs: something magnificent
Lies just beyond the dark.

Greatness lingers,
Veiled in mist. The path twists and bends,
Yet still, press on.
The storm will break—no tempest rages forever.
Rain pounds, wolves howl—
But move forward.

It's only water—
Wade through.
Step by step—
Wolves retreat,
Mountains bow,
Obstacles dissolve
Into pebbles beneath your feet.

Hold fast—
These detours are echoes
Of battles long won.
As you near your destiny,
Your resolve deepens,
Like roots anchoring
To the earth's molten core.

Each breath fortifies your ascent.
Find your rhythm,
In sync with the world's pulse.
Rise—
Upon the peak, the wind
Becomes your companion,
Triumphant.

Even lost among brambles,
Trust the wind—
It carried you here.
Turn back—
See the distance crossed,
The shadows trailing in your wake,
The storms you have conquered.

Each step, a thread
In the tapestry of your journey.
Time, a stitch
In the grand design.
Brush off the setbacks—
They are stones in the stream.

Move onward.
When the horizon reveals itself,
Raise your arms—
Feel triumph blaze
Within your veins.
Victory is not a distant summit,
But lies in every step.

Know this:

You've already won.
The path you tread
Ripples outward,
Guiding others
Through their storms.

So run—
Let your steps send waves forth,
Carving new paths
For those still seeking
The courage to begin.

A LOVE LIKE THIS

I found my way back to who I am,
But I did not arrive alone.
Even when I turned away,
Love never strayed.
Do we ever truly walk through life untouched, unaccompanied?

My mother, forever on her knees for me,
Her skin roughened, worn from years of prayer—
Yet she would say it was worth it—
Every moment, every sacrifice.

In youth, I believed I needed more—
Convinced the world had something grander to offer.
What I had seemed insufficient; salvation felt unnecessary.
So, I traded a blessed life for one cloaked in glitter,
Only to find the path far heavier than imagined.

I wept until my eyes burned raw,
Collapsed to my knees, broken time and again.
Now, as I look back, I see clearly—
A truth I was too blind to grasp:
My life was never mine to carry alone.
The burden, shouldered in solitude, made me smaller.
I believed strength dwelled within,
But He sought to make me whole.
He healed the voice I thought lost,
Gifting me a new song.

He saw me drowning in the tide,

He heard my cries in the dark.
When the storm howled, a beacon waited,
Yet I was too busy running, too proud to listen.
Had I paused, I would have seen—
His hand was always there,
Guiding, though not as I expected.

Where I was weak, He infused strength.
I said I would leave—my mother wept, and He stepped aside,
But neither truly left—
They stood by, steadfast.
One in spirit, the other, my eternal Guide.

Now I understand love for what it is:
It does not suffocate—it gives breath.
Love risks, it aches, but never controls.
Love waits, allowing you to labor through your own journey.
A life worth living is not measured by ease,
But by the trials that refine you,
The struggles that stretch you to grow.
When I finally turned my heart toward the heavens,
They smiled wide, welcoming me home.

Now I see—the love they gave was a gift,
And it's a blessing to know a love like this.

ALL I CAN DO

All I can do now
is look up,
into a sky that ripples like water,
where clouds drift, heavy with whispered secrets.
All I can say now is
thank you,
for the mercy that met me where I hid,
for the breath that fills this quiet space.
All I can be now is
the best of myself—
I can try, though I'll stumble,
trip over the shadows of old wounds,
push through thorns of shame,
walk barefoot over the glass of pain.
Trials will come,
storms of mirrors reflecting every fear,
but now I know:
all I have to do
is hold on to You—
the one thread that never frays.

I didn't choose to be lost,
but that's where I found myself,
wandering through a labyrinth of broken clocks,
time floating like feathers from my grasp.
I searched for answers in the mist,
thought You were silent
while I called Your name.
I asked for revelations,

for the sky to tear open
and spill stars,
but silence was all I heard.
I wasn't ready—
You did answer;
I just wasn't listening,
wasn't ready to hear
the quiet thunder beneath Your breath.

I filtered Your truth
through my own shattered lens,
believing I could trap infinity
in the palm of my hand.
I thought I could contain the only One,
who breathes galaxies to life,
whose whisper bends the rivers of time.
Even when I thought I had wisdom,
crafting philosophies from smoke,
I found only illusions—
ideas that slipped away
like dreams upon waking,
leaving me empty,
unable to fill the void
that gnawed at my soul.

I wandered down darker paths,
where the ground breathed,
the trees whispered my name,
but I couldn't outrun reality—
I couldn't outrun me.
I hated how my will
began to unravel, thread by thread,

how control slipped from my grasp
like sand through a broken hourglass.
I cried, I shouted,
kicked and screamed,
but You,
unshaken, stood like a mountain in the mist,
never letting me go.

I grew tired,
my hands heavy with the weight of nothing,
and now I release the struggle.
Your love is vast,
as deep as oceans dreaming beneath the earth.
Where missteps are met with indifference here,
You welcome me with open hands.
All You ever wanted was me,
and all I thought I wanted
was a version of myself
I had imagined,
but found only a shadow.

Now, I turn to Your grace,
a warmth that lifts like rising winds.
I look upon Your face,
though I see it only in the shimmer of things unseen.
I let myself feel a love
that cradles stars in its hands.
I can't count the ways
You've held me—
all the breaths and quiet moments,
the miracles I missed,
the countless times

You caught my fall before I knew I'd slipped.
I can't repay what Your Son did for me,
the sacrifice,
the blood that carved my name
into eternity,
so I could dance upon the clouds of heaven.

But I will live in wonder,
with eyes wide open to the mystery,
grateful as the sky breaks open
and pours light into my hands.
All I can do now
is look up.
All I can say now is
thank you,
for never letting go,
for making me so light
that now,
I can fall up.

EPILOGUE

Dear Friend,
Reflecting on my journey through shadows,
I see the strength born from each stumble,
The quiet resilience that took root within,
And the countless ways He carried me through.

Now, I cherish the small miracles,
The whispered assurances in the dark,
Knowing that in every struggle faced,
His unseen hand has been guiding me to the light.

Thank you for allowing me to share my story.
In truth, this is just the beginning.
The same hope awaits you, too.
Listen to that quiet voice.
A love like this,
Is a gift He'll give you, too.

And when you do,
Tell us what He did for you--
How He changed your life.

WORTH, NOT LESS

It's not panic—
Not exactly.
But it grips me all the same,
Tightening around my chest.
It's not you I've lost sight of—
Just the tears,
Distorting everything.

You were speaking,
Spilling words carelessly,
Then suddenly—
A silence so sharp it cuts,
Like snow falling,
Muting the world around us.

I thought we had more.
More time, more stories, more of us—
But that was my mistake.
I stared at my phone, hours bleeding into hours,
Like an addict, desperate for the next hit.
Turns out,
I wasn't part of your joke.

You let me dangle on every word—
Each pause an unspoken promise...
But—
You were cruel, weren't you?
Splashing me with hope, without direction,
Never saying go, but never letting me go.

A lone planet,
Floating in the remnants of what we lost,
Reflecting on the connection
We couldn't sustain.

And maybe—just maybe—
There's wisdom in this distance,
A chance to grow in the space we made.
I see now—
Some stars are meant to shine alone,
Some paths are best left untangled.

I'll keep drifting,
But with new understanding,
Embracing the space
That lets me grow.
In this vast expanse,
I'll find my own light,
Not just in what I've lost,
But in who I'll become.